i

Cover sculpture by Gyula Varosy Architect

VERBOTEN

Silencing The Individual

Max Hammer

Table of Contents

Initiation

"The unlearned is blind, although he can see"
Menander, c. 320 B.C.

Outside The Bubble

My qualifications for writing this book are not those of a scholar, but those of a participator, in the recent history of the rebirth of Europe, immediately after the Fall of the Berlin Wall. On my return to Canada, I was stunned by the utter lack of awareness, of the events surrounding the collapse of Communism. What is the reason for the apparent voter apathy, in our so called democracies? Ever since the inception of electronic media there has always been a tiny minority directing the conversation, which has been broadcast across entire continents, creating a top-down synthesis and distribution of information and opinion. When was the last time you remember having voted, in a referendum, on some controversial issue? We get to vote, once every four or five years, to elect a handful of leaders, who will then make all the decisions, without our direct involvement. This has left many with the feeling that we have little say, in the political decision making process. Only these tiny clubs of politicians, pundits and self-appointed experts, seemingly, have any right, to influence and power.

You may have noticed attitudinal changes, in our society, over the last few decades, if you are old enough. Homosexuality was illegal until the early 1970s. As late as the 1980s, gay marriage was considered an oxymoron by just about everyone. Women had always been expected to take care of the family and household, while the men had to go out, and work for the money that was needed, to feed their families, until about the same time, the early 1970s. Despite the fact that Adolf Hitler murdered six million Jews, in Poland, in the last two years of World War II, there was no Holocaust campaign, until the mid-1970s. Since the Cultural

Revolutions of the sixties, here in America, we have witnessed a decline in nuclear or traditional families, an increase in the divorce rate, an increase in abortions, an increase in the number of children born out of wedlock, a new bane of school shootings arrive in the 1990s, a massive rise in poverty, especially among African Americans, religions being replaced with new-age mysticism and the occult, three out of seven teenagers contemplating suicide and an increase in unemployment. In African American neighborhoods, we see that as the African American children grow up, through the public school system, half the young girls wind up going to college, while half the young boys wind up dead, in street violence or they end up in jail. Are these social changes naturally evolving adaptations to reality or, are they being driven by some deliberate influence?

Some of these new trends are also protected from critique. New hate-crime legislation and Political Correctness intimidate anyone, who wants to question the validity and justifiability of gay marriage, for example. And, what is Political Correctness, anyway?

There is rarely any discussion of what exactly, Hitler and Joseph Stalin were doing together, for the first two years of World War II. All historical documentaries made in English speaking countries, have WW II beginning basically, with the attack on Pearl Harbor, in 1941, while the real beginning of the war was in 1939, when Hitler and Stalin attacked Poland from both sides, and divided Poland into two halves, a National Socialist and an International Socialist half. But we only ever hear about how Hitler's National Socialists used the Blitzkrieg to attack Poland. There is hardly any mention of the fact that Stalin's Communists also attacked and killed many Poles and obediently sent train loads of Jews, to Hitler's Auschwitz, for two whole years.

If we are supposed to be so concerned, about the horrific mass-murder of six million Jews, in National Socialist concentration camps, in Poland, then why is there, as good as no mention, of the one hundred million or so murders of Gulag inmates, in the former Soviet Union, and also little mention of the forty or so million innocent people killed by Mao Tse Tung, during the great leap forward policy, in China, or the two million human souls killed in the rice fields of Cambodia, in the wake of the American defeat in Vietnam, in 1975? Our news media, no longer merely reports the facts. They have for a long time now, also decided which facts they want to talk about and which they want to keep from us. And our entertainment media is also no longer, merely about entertainment. It has become a propaganda machine, for conditioning, proselytizing and exclusively demonizing the right.

After the Second World War ended, there was a stream of blockbuster movies made to commiserate and commemorate the heroes and victims of that difficult conflict, against the totalitarian collective ideology of Adolf Hitler and his National Socialists. Hundreds of movies were made about this victory but, where are the movies commiserating and commemorating the heroes and victims of the Cold War against International Socialism or Communism, which was more recently won, by the United States and the Western democracies? Why is there, as good as no mention, of the crimes against humanity, committed by the Communists in Russia, China, Vietnam, Cambodia or Africa? When was the last time, you even heard the word "Communist", uttered on one of the major television

4

networks?

A business acquaintance of mine once asked me: "The German people produced such remarkable cultural milestones, Beethoven, Bach, high quality engineering, medical discoveries and seem to have produced a highly developed civilization. So why did these people vote for someone like Adolf Hitler?" We have to look at the map and remind ourselves of historic events around the 1930s. Hitler was elected with a slim margin in 1933 and was only able to form a government by joining in a coalition with another party. The banks had all collapsed, like dominoes, since the world found itself in the wake of the 1929 stock market crash, on Wall Street but, the more salient motive for Germans to swing over towards the Right, was the deliberate starvation of nine million people, in the Ukraine (on the other side of Poland, from Germany), by Joseph Stalin, in 1932. Moderate Germans were afraid of the Communists coming to power, in Germany, so they lurched over to the other extreme.

This planned famine in the Ukraine gets very little attention, in North America, except by Ukrainians and some other Eastern European refugees from Communism, who came over after World War II. Whatever the more complex explanation might be, we can certainly identify two big reasons for this omission. (1) Reason number one is that, the New Left (more on the New Left to follow) wants us to focus only, on the crimes against humanity, committed by the Right. They don't want us even to know about, the even bigger crimes against humanity, committed by the Communists. (2) The second weaker reason is that, the powers that be, in our own governments in the countries who were members of the Allies during World War II, are reluctant to bad-mouth a former ally, Russia, perhaps also, to avoid questions about culpability through guilt by association. After the war was over, Winston Churchill said: "We killed the wrong pig." He subsequently lost the English election of 1945, to Clement Attlee. The second reason is weaker because there is also a reluctance in the former Axis countries, Germany and Austria, for example, to mention crimes committed by Communists, even though Germany had only been allied with Russia, during the Hitler Stalin Pact, for two years, at the beginning of the war.

Hitler and the National Socialists came to power in Germany, as a reaction against the growing spread of Communism in Europe, particularly Russia and Eastern European countries like Hungary where Bela Kun had set up the short-lived Hungarian Soviet Republic, in the aftermath of the First World War, in 1919.

Some people think that Political Correctness is an innocuous, even humorous fashion of little consequence, which we needn't bother ourselves about. However, Political Correctness is in reality a euphemism for Cultural Marxism, which seeks to destroy Western Civilization and ultimately replace it with Communism. Marxists have taken control over the media in America – television and the film industry, around 1975, when America lost the Vietnam War and journalists successfully brought down an anti-Communist president, Richard Nixon. The American media was instrumental in the outcome of the Vietnam War by portraying U.S. efforts there as being futile and unjustified, despite the fact that Communists were clearly intent on taking over Vietnam. South-Vietnamese people were desperate to try to get on the last American helicopters, leaving the country, in 1974. Very few people want to live under Communism, especially when they do not get a choice, in the matter.

The news programs do not give us the back story, when they are reporting on some political event or issue. They merely beat around the bush, stay superficial and never mention who is to blame or why this event is even happening, unless the alleged perpetrators are right-wing. A good example of this is the diametrically lopsided coverage given to the Apartheid regime of South Africa, on the one hand, and the coverage given to the Rwandan Massacre of 1994, in Africa, on the other hand. A world-wide campaign was relentlessly promoted against Apartheid, including rock concerts staring celebrity luminaries, for decades until the African National Congress party finally took over the country, on 27 April, 1994. In this same year, the Hutus killed the Tutsis but, what the motivation was, the media seemingly, could not even have cared less. The Hutus, who fancied themselves as the oppressed underdogs, it turns out, were inspired by Karl Marx and the French Revolution but, instead of guillotines, they had to make due, with machetes. Tutsis were always more congenial towards their French colonizers than the Hutu, therefore they evolved to become the favored people for jobs and seemed to enjoy more benefits than the Hutus. The Marxist dominated United Nations, famously stood by and ignored the genocide, as it was unfolding. Nine hundred thousand men, women and children were hacked to death, by these Marxist inspired Socialists.

Instead of bringing us stories about the dramatic events of recent history leading up to the collapse of Communism, Hollywood only wants to focus on the dysfunctional American family, the glories of feminism and gay marriage or waste our precious time with stupid blockbusters based on comic book characters or infantile cartoons. Only left-wing ideas are allowed to be explored by the big and little screens, which are fed by Hollywood leftists like Larry Gelbart, Norman Lear, Woody Allen and Rob Reiner. If it is found out that, a screenwriter or actor has conservative views, he or she will lose their job in Hollywood, now controlled by a left-wing black list. The same people who whine about the black listing of writers in Hollywood during the 1950s, are now availing themselves of exactly the same tactic.

You are no longer allowed to voice a conservative point of view, such as, that gay marriage is wrong and will deteriorate our religious values, even more than they already have been or, that abortion has taken the lives of millions of Americans, who could otherwise have provided a domestic youth that now has to be replaced, with foreign immigration, thanks to Feminism. Free speech is no longer acceptable in Canada, where someone criticizing gays defining societal standards, could even be accused of hate crime and go to jail, for trying to speak out. If we do not have free speech then, we are no longer living in a free country. On a recent Meet The Press, in connection with the controversy over new religious freedom laws in Indiana, some of the pundits joked that if only we could get rid of everyone over fifty then, we would have no more problems. This is not funny. The left can make jokes about exterminating people with conservative opinions, without fear of being accused of Hate Crime, as long as they are the ones, directing the conversation. This one-sided conversation is what is meant by Political Correctness and it may also be referred to as Cultural Marxism.

The purpose of all this is to create a collective political consciousness that only accommodates a single ideological point of view, or direction. Everyone must march in lock-step, in one direction. Conservatives must be silenced and ultimately there should be only one political party: a Marxist dictatorship is what the ultimate goal of the New Left is.

Basically, Old Leftists were Marxists prior to the First World War who pursued a political ideology based on economics and class warfare. The New Leftists are new Marxists, since World War I, who are pursuing their ideology based on cultural warfare, such as the destruction of Christianity, traditional values and Western Civilization, the destruction of which, was also one of the ultimate goals of Karl Marx. Their centers of power have eventually become the colleges, universities, government regulatory agencies and the mainstream media, movies and television.

The new left's early television sitcoms were politically obvious, overt and crude; shows like All In The Family and M.A.S.H. Recently they have developed shows that are more subtle and covert, such as Friends and Glee. I personally enjoyed the sitcom Friends and did not have a whisper of a suspicion, that there was a Marxist writing the lines, until I read Ben Shapiro's mercurial book, Primetime Propaganda, which drills into the Hollywood left, where he interviewed Martha Kaufman, the creator and writer of the series. She explained that the purpose of Friends was to persuade young *white* women that they do not need a man and all they needed was to live in a collective of friends, to be happy and stay emotionally and sexually satisfied. She also proclaimed herself to be a radical Marxist feminist.

Our mainstream media also uses half-truths to

deceive us into accepting policies which we really don't want. Obamacare is one of the most shining examples of this trick of the stealth-left who seem to be in control of the television and print media. Universal or free health care equals "no frills" or "economy" health care. The media is only showing us one side of the coin that free healthcare should be our right and that it has no justifiable rebuttal. What the mainstream media neglects to talk about is that, one doesn't go to a socialist country to get a treatment for a difficult medical problem, such as a gunshot wound to the foot or a brain tumor because they have neither the talent nor the technical facility, to deal with these more complicated problems. In the case of a gunshot wound to the foot, the doctors in a no frills healthcare system might simply decide to amputate your foot, whereas in the United States, doctors are equipped to fix your foot without having to resort to amputation. That is why many people with serious medical problems chose to go to the U.S., from Canada, even though the healthcare system in Canada is ostensibly "free".

A government managed healthcare system is really a Marxian price control scheme. In such a system, doctors wind up effectively, as employees of the state, who are only permitted to receive a specific amount of money, for a particular procedure or operation, according to a regulatory remuneration code book. The tendency for doctors' behavior under such a limited income scenario, is to work as few hours as possible, since there is no incentive for over-time effort and no allowance for innovation or creativity. Doctors drop their stethoscopes at 5:00 pm and go home. This leads to a perceived shortage of physicians and increased waiting times for the patients.

You cannot compare the design of a motor vehicle to

the evolution of our modern free market economic system. Only a finite thing like a building, airplane or car, can be designed or drawn up on a drafting table or on a computer monitor to be iteratively printed out, as a set of schematic drawings for frequent phases of study and refinement. The economy is far too complex to be grasped, even by a genius like Stephen Hawking, let alone by a self-proclaimed economist like Karl Marx.

Social engineers of the twentieth century, inspired by the Newtonian mathematics of nineteenth century mechanical physics, became deluded by this fallacy. They thought that an egalitarian re-distribution of wealth and production was merely a matter of careful analysis and design. The economy was seen as being a complex machine, whose moving parts one needed only study, in order to be able to make the necessary improvements.

The reality is that the economy does not obey simple mechanical laws, which can be easily grasped. It is a complex dynamic system of communication and behavior, that is continually attended to, by literally all of the participants, however small. It mercilessly rejects paths that lead nowhere, or don't bring anything. It has evolved over thousands of years and has been influenced by millions of intelligent people. It is so finely articulated and complex that, millions of people can be sustained at a high standard of living while interacting with each other on opposite ends of cities, territories and even the globe itself, without the need for these people to know one another, or share the same political views or religious beliefs.

The economy is like other similar dynamic systems, such as language, religion, law and art. No one person, or educated nucleus of individuals "designed" the English language. It is an evolving system of vocabulary, syntax, grammar, poetry, plays and novels that has had a very large number of contributors, over many centuries. Ludwig von Mises and Friedrich August von Hayek, founders of the Austrian School of Economics, thought that a special name should be given to these kinds of dynamic systems of human ingenuity, so they coined the term "catallaxy".

Capitalism is not a theory, in contrast to Marxism or communism. Capitalism, or more appropriately, Free-Market Enterprise, is a dynamically evolving system of behavior that started thousands of years ago. It works because it has evolved through trial and error, over a long time. Free-Market Enterprise, Roman Law, Spanish and Judaism, these are all guidance systems that most people recognize as being useful for hosting complex spiritual and material interactions between large numbers of human beings with disparate agendas.

Environmentalists, feminists and Marxists are going up against this train of human experience. The burden of proof rests upon the shoulders of those who propose a new idea, and nobody should automatically accept these agitators' premises, prior to such empirical proof being demonstrated. Many conservatives are confounded by these renegades; they know deep down, that some of these new ideas are wrong, but find it difficult to identify the arguments with which to counter them.

The purpose of this book is to shed light on this siege from within and, to make as many people as possible aware of the predicament, in which we find ourselves.

M. Hammer, July 4, 2015.

Chapter 1

Political Correctness

The dishonest does not escape the punishment,
he just delays it.
Publilius Syrus, 1st c. B.C.

Thought Control

Karl Marx predicted an ultimate class revolution, in the future, that would wrest power away from the ruling class and give it over to the working class. Marx was a German philosopher who lived from 1818 until 1883. He was influenced by Georg Hegel and he is considered, by many historians, to be the father of modern Communism. In 1843, Marx was ordered out of Prussia because of the contents of his newspaper Die Neue Rheinische Zeitung, which was funded by his blue-blood wife, Jenny von Westphalen. Marx wrote, among other things, that the ruling class needs to be exterminated, in order for a better society to be created. It was a form of so called hate speech, by today's moral standards. He was given the choice, by the police, of either remaining in Prussia and being tried for treason or, leaving Prussia, never to return again. The punishment for treason, in those days was the death penalty. In his final publication, which he had printed in red ink, Marx wrote that millions of people who were not ready for socialism, because they hadn't evolved through capitalism yet, would have to perish, in the coming revolutionary holocaust. He was the first known literary luminary, to advocate for mass-murder, in writing. Marx packed up his family and their belongings and went off to Paris, France, in October of 1843.

All European radicals and socialists looked upon France as the progressive hope of the world, during the first half of the 19th century, since the people there, had gone through the ten year long, bloody and horrific French Revolution, a few decades earlier, from 1790 until 1800, and had exterminated practically every member of the entire ruling class. Actually all the nobility had been killed off, in the first three years and, it wasn't until this goal had been completed, that the real terror started, under Maximilian Robespierre, the leader of the revolution. Many regular working class people were being accused of loyalty to the nobility, arrested and sent to the guillotine, allowing the blood, not only to continue flowing but, to flow more vigorously. A reign of terror descended on the revolution, which lasted on, until the execution of Robespierre himself, by guillotine. Robespierre was a paranoid tyrant, who continually felt that he had to expand the radius of people to blame. He was a kind of forerunner, to Joseph Stalin.

It is therefore possible to make the case, that during his stay in France, Karl Marx really learned about Communism, having been inspired and greatly influenced by the legacy of the French Revolution, in addition to having witnessed the Communes and their inhabitants, who called themselves "Communares". He wanted to see a French style revolution, all across the globe. Marx also met the German socialist Friedrich Engels in this exile, in a Parisian Cafe, where radicals and socialists gathered to confer, on what policies, directions and philosophy the new society should pursue. Between Marx's death in 1883 and the beginning of the First World War, in 1914, many people fell in love with the rhetoric and narratives of Karl Marx and Friedrich Engels, and these people came to be known as Marxists.

As the storm clouds gathered in the run-up to the First World War, Marxists were hoping that this would be a perfect opportunity, for the great worker's revolution, throughout Europe, which had been predicted by their notorious messiah. When the war did come, the workers put on their uniforms and went off to the battlefields, to fight for King and country instead. The much anticipated revolution failed to materialize. Immediately after the First World War, Marxists felt betrayed by the working class, whom they had fought so hard for, in all their writings and speeches. This gave rise to the so called "New Left" wave of Marxists. This new strain of Marxism decided not to pursue the economic class warfare philosophy of Karl Marx but rather, to re-define Marxism in cultural terms; Cultural Marxism or what we today know as Political Correctness, a euphemism for Cultural Marxism.

The First World War did furnish the opportunity for the Communists to revolt, first in Russia in 1917, and then in Germany, in 1918. The German Emperor Wilhelm II had to flee to the Netherlands. The Russian military was greatly weakened, due to the fighting in the First World War, and was consequently no longer feared by Stalin, Trotsky, Lenin and their followers, and so they were free to take over the country and put Karl Marx's ideas into practice. The German army was not so decimated, therefore the German Communists could not take over Germany completely. However they did reign in power, with the SPD (Sozial-democratische Partei Deutschlands) in Berlin, and did help to promulgate the surrender to France. This surrender came as a shock, to the fighting men in the trenches, who felt that Germany was winning the war against the allies, particularly since Russia had resigned from the war, due to its revolution. A young lieutenant, Adolf Hitler, was one of these soldiers, who felt betrayed by the Communist politicians, in Berlin.

A very wealthy young Marxist heir, to a large South American grain plantation fortune, Felix Weil, (1898-1975) decided to create a foundation for the development of a Marxist institute, in Frankfurt, Germany in 1922. Soon the idea to call it a Marxist institute was abandoned for a less controversial sounding, Institut Fuer Sozial Forschung or Institute for Social Research. Carl Gruenberg was the founding director, in 1923. The first order of business for these new leftists, was to find a new direction and a new constituency for Marxist ideas, which did not rely on economic arguments. New surrogates had to be sought by the New Left, to replace the unreliable working class.

Who could be used, as a large enough group, to provide the necessary energy required, for a major revolution? The first obvious group, which came to the mind of psychoanalyst and member Erich Fromm, was women, who represented half the population of any given society. He and Herbert Marcuse coined the expression "Gender Politics". Feminism was to become a major surrogate for Marxism and it would also later be weaponized as Militant Feminism.

In 1930, Max Horkheimer replaced Carl Gruenberg as director and wrote Critical Theory. What is Critical Theory? One might assume that it is some kind of hypothesis which is used to question societal values and appraise their usefulness, or something along similar lines. But Critical Theory is in reality nothing more than to criticize every good thing in Western culture, including the institution of marriage, the family, the authority of parents, the wholesomeness of virtue and obedience to the law, objective debate, religious traditions and patriotism, until there is nothing left standing. He criticized bourgeois society for it's "militarism", "economic disruptions", "environmental crises" and the "poverty of mass culture".

Anything which does not align with Marxism is wrong, according to Critical Theory. And it was written in a cryptic language which a normal reader will find very difficult to understand. It is really a kind of sweeping intellectually abstract poetry or, picture language.

The goal of Critical Theory was to negate anything which questions Marxism. In other words, you are not allowed to have any other opinions or beliefs, other than Marxism. This is the essence of totalitarian thought. And modern Political Correctness, as the name suggests, accepts only one direction of thought: Socialism or ultimately, Communism. Other companions of this hive of critique, of our Western civilization were, Theodor Adorno, Herbert Marcuse, Friedrich Pollock, and Otto Kirchheimer, among many others. Unfortunately for America, they decided to pack their bags and move to New York, in 1933, getting help and support from Columbia University. Why the move? Because Adolf Hitler came to power in 1933 and these Communists were afraid that they might be arrested, if they didn't leave Germany.

The founder of the Italian Communist Party, Antonio Gramsci (1891-1937) had been imprisoned by Benito Musolini, since 1926. In prison he wrote his The Prison Notebooks, in which he called out for, capturing the culture. This was his remedy for Capitalism. Marxists should infiltrate and take control of the institutions, the church, the schools, on all levels, the print media, newspapers and magazines, and the broadcast media of radio and the medium of motion pictures and plays. He thought that if Marxists could get control of these cultural institutions then, they could manipulate how people thought, by defining the vocabulary and directing all conversation. This is basically what we are enduring today, in America and other Western countries, in the movies, on television and in many magazines and newspapers. Education and media were, and still are the most important targets, for infiltration and control, by the Marxists.

Herbert Marcuse (1898-1979), who came from the Frankfurt School, eventually settled in the University of California, Brandeis, where he taught sociology. He preached total sexual freedom, where no act was considered too perverted. For example, children should have sex with adults, and homosexuality should be considered normal and even healthy. These Marxists had begun to teach in American universities, in the mid-1930s, so by the mid-1960s, they had had three decades, within which to prepare the groundwork of campus culture, that would eventually motivate the students to attempt a revolution, which we know today as, the student revolts of the sixties, or the Counterculture Hippie Movement. The young people of this era had neither the organizational skills, intellectual preparation or political overview, to pull off the coordinated demonstrations and violent campus riots, that ensued, and threatened the peace, in the United States, during these tumultuous times. But the old Marxist intellectuals, who were themselves, by then, in their sixties, certainly did, not only possess those skills but, had the time and financial support to persuade and organize the students, to mount these riots.

All of these Marxist theorists who arrived in New York, in 1933, were immediately given teaching jobs, in Columbia University except for a few who decided to go to California. Marcuse was interested in using sex to undermine the religious traditions and institutions, such as marriage, in order to erode the moral foundations of Western culture. All forms of sexual deviancy, pornography and perversion should not only be allowed but, they should be encouraged. Homosexuality should also be allowed to flourish, in the open. For thirty years, Marcuse in California and the other Marxists in other colleges across North America, worked to cultivate a new ethos on campus which was defiant of the traditional values, of the rest of American society. By 1963, when John F. Kennedy was assassinated and Lyndon Johnson overtook the prosecution of the "Vietnam Crisis" (the Johnson administration didn't want to admit that they were in a war) an opportunity presented itself to galvanize resistance to this war, and put the now critical mass of indoctrinated students, into revolutionary mode.

What the media portrayed as a student revolution, was in fact a movement that was three decades in the making and directed by old German Marxist professors, who were coaching and instructing those students in the art and craft of rebellion. All the memorable witty phrases of the 1960s so called Hippie movement, such as "Make love, not war", "Don't trust anyone over 30" and referring to policemen as "Fascist Pigs", were carefully thought out by Herbert Marcuse, who was born in 1898! He provided the intellectual framework of the Cultural Revolution in books such as "Counterrevolution and Revolt"-1969, "Reason and Revolution: Hegel and the Rise of Social Theory"-1941, "Eros and Civilization: A Philosophical Enquiry into Freud"-1955, in which he promotes every kind of sexual perversion imaginable, and "A Critique of Pure Tolerance"-1965, in which he argues that not all political points of view should be tolerated, only those that lead to Socialism, which is the final keystone in the foundation of, what would later come to be known as Political Correctness. This seminal guru mastermind of the Flower Power movement, was a 71 year old Marxist professor, in the year 1969, who brainwashed his young California students, to revolt against "The Establishment", a curse word, for our free society.

During the 1950s, America was able to hold the Communists at bay, in the Korean War. South Korea had been successfully re-acquired by General Douglas MacArthur, after an initial invasion and overrunning by the Communists, in 1950. The Communists in China, who were supporting the North-Vietnamese didn't want a repeat of Korea, in Vietnam, so they got hold of their Marxist helpers in the United States, through Soviet and K.G.B. contacts, to organize anti-war protests within the U.S. Many Soviet agents had infiltrated the U. S. during the Second World War, after Russia had become allies with the U. S., in the fight against Hitler's Germany. One of the primary goals of these 1960s student riots, was to try to persuade the American public, of the futility of fighting against Communism in Vietnam. Male students burned their draft cards, let down their hair, tuned in, turned on to drugs and dropped out, to the melodic intonation of acid rock. Ultimately, America was defeated in the Vietnam War, due to a reduction in will power, on the part of the American people, which was engineered by the media, which had successfully toppled an anti-Communist president, Richard Nixon, in the Watergate scandal, in 1974.

The Russian K.G.B. had always been active in Western countries, including the United States. And the nature of their activity, according to Yuri Bezmenov, a former K.G.B. agent, was to do many things to undermine and destabilize society, that were all perfectly legal, such as printing disinformation pamphlets, helping various civil rights organizations and supporting several movements which were thought to be potentially, anti-capitalist or socialist, in nature. It had nothing to do with the cliché cloak and dagger James Bond espionage activities, portrayed in Hollywood movies. Of the entire KGB budget, 15% was spent on what one might call espionage activities, while 85% was spent on psychological warfare and subversion activities. However, subversion is a two way street. The subverter must have a receptive target, for the subversion to be successful. This was to be provided by the New Left and their political correctness conditioning propaganda.

No one should be allowed to debate any issue unless they were of the Left-Wing persuasion. This was also known as Negation Theory according to Marcuse and Theodore Adorno. It is nothing less than the elimination of free speech, in an ostensibly open society.

The half a dozen or so cultural movements became surrogates for the New Left to be used to stoke a revolution, instead or in lieu of the unreliable working class, to undermine the cultural foundation of the West: Christianity. This is the number one obstacle to Socialism and Communism, in the world. The following is a list of movements which had been ideologically weaponized:

Political Correctness = Cultural Marxism

Apparatus Promoting Movements

Academic   - Marxist professors influencing students' ideological thinking.

Media   - Hollywood films, television and magazines conditioning public oppinion.

Regulatory - Government agencies increasing permissions required, relentlessly.

Political   - Organized Marxists infiltrating mainstream institutions.

Movement	Pretext	Targets	Began
Feminist	Gender Fairness	Family	
Environmental	Pollution	Freedom and Industry	
Civil Rights	Racism	Tranquility	1960s
Labor	Workers' Welfare	Economy	
Sexual Liberation	Behavioral Equality	Christianity	
Peace	Anti-War	Defence	
Multicultural	Cultural Equivalence	Western Culture	1970s
Pride	Hate-Crime	Free Speech	

23

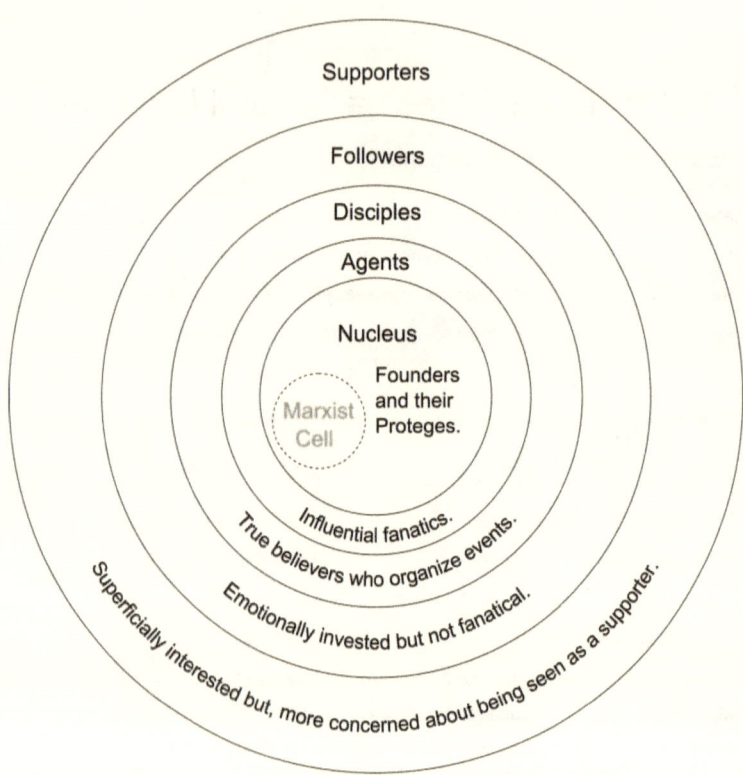

Supporters

Followers

Disciples

Agents

Nucleus

Founders and their Proteges.

Marxist Cell

Influential fanatics.

True believers who organize events.

Emotionally invested but not fanatical.

Superficially interested but, more concerned about being seen as a supporter.

Anatomy of a Movement

Feminism vs. the traditional Family (remove the father)

Environmentalism vs. Industry/Business

Gay Activism vs. Christianity

Drug Revolution vs. Prudence and Discipline

Sexual Revolution vs. Decency and Health

Modern Art (Ugliness) vs. American Culture (Purpose)

Civil Rights Revolution vs. American Institutions

Multiculturalism vs. Western Culture

"We are going to corrupt the West so much, that it stinks"
Willi Muenzenberg (Frankfurt School)

Since about 1963 America and other countries in the West have lost their moral compass. After the assassination of President John F. Kennedy the F.B.I. raided a Communist Party of U.S.A headquarters in Miami and found a 1958 K.G.B. memo listing a series of 45 goals for the C.P.U.S.A., which is reprinted below:

From "The Naked Communist," by Dr. Cleon Skousen

Communist Goals (1963) Congressional Record--
Appendix, pp. A34-A35 January 10, 1963

1. U.S. acceptance of coexistence as the only alternative to atomic war.

2. U.S. willingness to capitulate in preference to engaging in atomic war.

3. Develop the illusion that total disarmament [by] the United States would be a demonstration of moral strength.

4. Permit free trade between all nations regardless of Communist affiliation and regardless of whether or not items could be used for war.

5. Extension of long-term loans to Russia and Soviet satellites.

6. Provide American aid to all nations regardless of Communist domination.

7. Grant recognition of Red China. Admission of Red China to the U.N.

8. Set up East and West Germany as separate states in spite of Khrushchev's promise in 1955 to settle the German question by free elections under supervision of the U.N.

9. Prolong the conferences to ban atomic tests because the United States has agreed to suspend tests as long as negotiations are in progress.

10. Allow all Soviet satellites individual representation in

the U.N.

11. Promote the U.N. as the only hope for mankind. If its charter is rewritten, demand that it be set up as a one-world government with its own independent armed forces. (Some Communist leaders believe the world can be taken over as easily by the U.N. as by Moscow. Sometimes these two centers compete with each other as they are now doing in the Congo.)

12. Resist any attempt to outlaw the Communist Party.

13. Do away with all loyalty oaths.

14. Continue giving Russia access to the U.S. Patent Office.

15. Capture one or both of the political parties in the United States.

16. Use technical decisions of the courts to weaken basic American institutions by claiming their activities violate civil rights.

17. Get control of the schools. Use them as transmission belts for socialism and current Communist propaganda. Soften the curriculum. Get control of teachers' unions. Put the party line in textbooks.

18. Gain control of all student newspapers.

19. Use student riots to foment public protests against

programs or organizations which are under Communist attack.

20. Infiltrate the press. Get control of book-review assignments, editorial writing, policy-making positions.

21. Gain control of key positions in radio, TV, and motion pictures.

22. Continue discrediting American culture by degrading all forms of artistic expression. An American Communist cell was told to "eliminate all good sculpture from parks and buildings, substitute shapeless, awkward and meaningless forms."

23. Control art critics and directors of art museums. "Our plan is to promote ugliness, repulsive, meaningless art."

24. Eliminate all laws governing obscenity by calling them "censorship" and a violation of free speech and free press.

25. Break down cultural standards of morality by promoting pornography and obscenity in books, magazines, motion pictures, radio, and TV.

26. Present homosexuality, degeneracy and promiscuity as "normal, natural, healthy."

27. Infiltrate the churches and replace revealed religion with "social" religion. Discredit the Bible and emphasize the need for intellectual maturity, which does not need a "religious crutch."

28. Eliminate prayer or any phase of religious expression in the schools on the ground that it violates the principle of "separation of church and state."

29. Discredit the American Constitution by calling it inadequate, old-fashioned, out of step with modern needs, a hindrance to cooperation between nations on a worldwide basis.

30. Discredit the American Founding Fathers. Present them as selfish aristocrats who had no concern for the "common man."

31. Belittle all forms of American culture and discourage the teaching of American history on the ground that it was only a minor part of the "big picture." Give more emphasis to Russian history since the Communists took over.

32. Support any socialist movement to give centralized control over any part of the culture--education, social agencies, welfare programs, mental health clinics, etc.

33. Eliminate all laws or procedures which interfere with the operation of the Communist apparatus.

34. Eliminate the House Committee on Un-American Activities.

35. Discredit and eventually dismantle the FBI.

36. Infiltrate and gain control of more unions.

37. Infiltrate and gain control of big business.

38. Transfer some of the powers of arrest from the police to social agencies. Treat all behavioral problems as psychiatric disorders which no one but psychiatrists can understand [or treat].

39. Dominate the psychiatric profession and use mental health laws as a means of gaining coercive control over those who oppose Communist goals.

40. Discredit the family as an institution. Encourage promiscuity and easy divorce.

41. Emphasize the need to raise children away from the negative influence of parents. Attribute prejudices, mental blocks and retarding of children to suppressive influence of parents.

42. Create the impression that violence and insurrection are legitimate aspects of the American tradition; that students and special-interest groups should rise up and use ["]united force["] to solve economic, political or social problems.

43. Overthrow all colonial governments before native populations are ready for self-government.

44. Internationalize the Panama Canal.

45. Repeal the Connally reservation so the United States

cannot prevent the World Court from seizing jurisdiction [over domestic problems. Give the World Court jurisdiction] over nations and individuals alike.

Notes

Chapter 2

The Environmental Pretext

"The most corrupt state has the most laws."
Tacitus, 117 A.D.

Green Superstitions

The left has been using platitudes and scare tactics about the human condition for a long time. The station point for Karl Marx's theoretical perspective was taken in the future. He looked back at the present from his ultimate vantage point of a distant future Utopian superman, to illustrate all of the shortcomings of our current "medieval" existence, and social orders. In 1967, the Club of Rome, a "union of concerned scientists" presented us with a propaganda documentary entitled "The Limits to Growth", which relied heavily on computer models to make projections about pollution, population growth and shortages, into the future.

"This time it was not the Third World but the world itself: nature personified as a new proletariat gagging on the effluents and effects of industry. Every sign of commerce began to signify a rising residue of environmental burdens: additives and surfactants, plastics and phosphates, x-rays and electromagnetic waves, PCBs and EDB, nuclear leaks and toxic wastes. Their computers drew trend lines representing the emission of poisons into the atmosphere, the population growth, the precipitous explosion of industry, the shortages of food and crude oil and they would all rise exponentially, take a sharp turn for the worse in the 1980s, and finally culminate in a coincidental spike in the year 2000."

George Gilder, The Spirit of Enterprise

This was when we would run out of everything. We would all die of starvation, or kill each other over food. Those of us who were left, would need gas masks in order to be able to breath, as fresh air would no longer be available. Evidence of the mood of these final years of the hippie age of Aquarius, is the Hollywood produced sci-fi thriller Soylent Green starring Charlton Heston, depicting a future that had run out of food and was dependent on the processing of human cadavers for it's very sustenance. This hallucinogenic liberal enthusiasm for environmental doom took hold of our ethos, fifty years ago!

When Hollywood isn't doing a sequel, it's making a remake. The year 2000 came and went. The y2k hysteria also turned out to be a flop. The prescience of Orwell's warning of the coming of a global Socialism, by the year 1984, may have been inaccurate but, the obverse seemed to come true, five years later, as the colossus of Communism collapsed, in 1989. It is astonishing, how little is made of such a dramatic and epic event, in our own time. One would think there is plenty of material for at least a couple of Hollywood blockbusters, there. But, no, we need to revisit the aging baby-boomer's left-wing agenda of healing mother earth of the crimes of Capitalism.

The real story is of course, that the right wing won the argument. So what can the left wing, at the controls of media do? Pretend it isn't so. Keep making remakes, and hope the right goes away. And so, we are living in a World War II time-warp ethos and indulging in old hippie paranoias. Instead of studying the mass of evidence that is collecting dust, in Communist archives, in the former Warsaw Pact countries, of mass murder and why the socialist experiment went wrong, we close our eyes, and pretend it never happened. Our attention is drawn to what the left wing wants us to see; how capitalism is taking us on a false course, despite the obvious fact that the free market has stood us in good stead, throughout a century of socialist barbarism.

35

The Sky is Falling!

Forty years ago, we went through a doom and gloom hypochondria, in the 1970's, kicked off by the Club of Rome's "The Limits to Growth" paradigm. It predicted exponential growth in all the maladies of industrialization: pollution, the greenhouse effect and the exhaustion of our limited oil reserves. By the 1980's, we were told by their expert's computer model projections, pollution would be so bad that we would all need gas masks, to be able to survive in our cities.

"At the opening of the October 1973 war in Israel, on Oct 17, Arab oil-producing nations announced they would begin cutting back on oil exports to Western nations and Japan; the result was a total embargo that lasted until March, 1974 and caused oil prices to quadruple. Rationing and gunfights at gas lines, ensued in the U.S. Experts in Harvard and the energy guru of the day, Walter Levy forecast doom for western society, and Charles Lindblom of Yale summed up the mood in *Politics and Markets*, in 1972:

"Relentlessly accumulating evidence suggests that human life on the planet is headed for catastrophe."

The only way to avert it, he maintained, was through imposition of central planning. Our economies gasped. The U.S. government established the Department of Energy, a synfuels corporation was set up, the U.S. Congress enacted a national speed limit, a law against the use of natural gas in new utilities and, a complex scheme of price controls and entitlements, on both oil and gas. Washington started subsidizing windmills, solar cells, insulation and "gasohol" while penalizing the use of petroleum. But as the 1970s progressed, the gloom seemed to grow worse and worse. On Feb 15, 1974, U.S. gas stations

36

threatened to close because of federal fuel policies. By 1979, OPEC again doubled it's price on oil. [In this year also, the Green Party of Germany was officially founded, in Bonn.]

In Canada the government sharply increased energy taxes. In the fall of 1972, the National Energy Board of Canada issued a stark warning that, oil and gas production was pushing near it's limits and could no longer keep up with the demand. The experts and bureaucrats were painting a picture of finite resources that was abetted by a new bane, stagflation in the economy and communist expansion in Asia, Central America and Africa."

George Gilder, The Spirit Of Enterprise

Against this backdrop of malaise, John Masters, a 47 year old, unemployed explorer from Tulsa, Oklahoma, went into the mountains of Alberta, when all other companies were leaving. Armed solely with a concept and experience gathered at Kerr McGee, he discovered an immense natural gas basin at Elmworth, British Columbia, which stretched into Alberta. This new basin contained 400 trillion cubic feet of natural gas, six times all of the known reserves in Canada, at the time. He single handedly solved the energy crisis for us, in North America. He ushered in a new age of discovery for the oil companies, and ultimately, the OPEC nations relaxed their prices during the 1980s.

The real innovations and solutions come from individuals with a vision, not from entrenched bureaucracies blinded by their own gathered expert knowledge and data.

Communism and socialism seemed to be viable alternatives to capitalism during the cold war, especially during the 1960's and 1970's, at least in the popular media and in intellectual circles, in the Western democracies. It was the Age of Aquarius, flower power, feminism, acid rock, the Viet-Nam War and Watergate. Left wing political parties such as the NDP in Canada, the front party of the communists, which was once known as the CCF (Cooperative Commonwealth Federation), claiming to represent the working class, were able to reference their ideological bearings and orient their agenda, on various issues, in relation to these defining sets of, then seemingly, current edicts or precepts.

After the collapse of communism in the country of its origin, the Soviet Union or Russia, the currency and credibility of these edicts suffered a stunning blow. There has been a major re-alignment of ideological values since. In our culture "business" is the new panacea and the environment is the new issue that the left wing is struggling to sustain a monopoly over. Even this cause has become interesting to right wing political parties.

Inveterate Fallacies

"Economists from Aristotle to Marx have all fallen prey to the fallacy of assuming that objects or services possess a calculable intrinsic value or cost. It was assumed that by an act of measurement, people established the value of a product or service, and then, sought to exchange it for a product or service of equivalent value. It wasn't until David Hume, the British Currency School and John Stuart Mill came along that, this lamentable defect was noticed."

Ludwig von Mises, Human Action

The basis of modern economics is the recognition that, it is precisely the disparity in the value of the objects or services offered, that results in their being exchanged. Beauty is in the eye of the beholder. An example of this would be; if a young hockey player who possesses a light saber toy and his Star Wars fan cousin, not interested in sports, who owns a Buffalo Sabers jersey, decide to make the trade of the century. Each partner is exchanging something of almost no value, for something of almost inestimable value. Both are happy after the trade. Clearly, these objects have no intrinsic value at all. The value is attached to things by people driven by ethics, subjective desires, beliefs and other motivations.

Some people believe that 110,000 murders are being committed every year in Canada, by feminist agitated, young women who want sex in the city, without responsibility. What is the dollar value of this ongoing mass murder? Should young women considering abortion, be made to buy murder credits, that could be donated to the families of victims of crime, to offset this iniquity? What dollar value do we place on one human being?

20 million inmates in concentration camps and forced labor coal mines, in China, are working without pay, for the purpose of erecting one dirty coal plant a week, providing us with cheap products and wiping out our economy. Perhaps we should insist that the Chinese government invest in mass murder credits for every dissident they kill. Since carbon and mass murder are disparate values, should we consider exchanging mass murder credits for carbon credits?

Al Gore is an aging, over-weight former presidential candidate, who needs something to help him stay relevant. Global climate change is his crutch, that he is using to cling to the limelight and his wealthy allies in Hollywood, gave him a helping hand, by propping up his self-serving computer graphic image enhanced, re-make of the Club of Rome's 1970 movie, "The Limits to Growth". Unfortunately, he got carried away by his own delusional hype and is now turning into a modern day "repent your sins, the Day of Judgment is at hand" fear monger. It is astonishing to see how gullible people can be.

Carbon credits are a farce anyway, because China and India are not required by Kyoto to put a cap on their carbon emissions. Instead of pointing the finger of blame and punishing particular businesses for their inadvertent contributions to pollution, while serving us, the consumers, why not focus on solving the pollution problem? Incentives should be devised to be given to companies who make important strides in the direction of a cleaner environment.

Coercion is inimical to a free society and a flourishing economy. Only a flourishing economy can sustain the true burden of what people consider to be vital and desirable.

The Green party continually tries to push the notion that the "true costs" can be calculated and should be added to the price of energy. Karl Marx used the same reasoning to lower the prices of goods and services, in order to promote a more egalitarian society. The only way we can achieve clean energy is by the use of sophisticated technologies such as nuclear, for example. But sophisticated technologies require, as a pre-requisite, a healthy economy, with low taxation and a high degree of incentives. Poor socialist countries are the worst polluters, while rich, free market countries are the only ones that can develop products such as the hybrid automobile. Using a policy of punishment, raising taxes to coerce cleaner behavior will ultimately lead to poverty and an inability to produce the sophisticated clean energy technologies that we need.

On Thursday, the 9th of November, 1989, the Left lost the major political contest of the twentieth century, the Cold War, when the Berlin Wall finally fell. Yet they still pervade in our media, like bad weather. Since the old socialist rhetoric no longer enjoys the same legitimacy or currency, they have had need of a new agenda, with which to proselytize young intellectuals.

    The esoteric think tank of the Left, in Germany – Heinrich Böll and three radical students, saw the writings of Alexandr Solzhenitsyn, when his book The Gulag Archipelago was first published in 1973, and realized that it would have difficulty recruiting young people, in the future.

    The collapse of the Soviet Union, the evil empire, that was spreading communism, for over seventy years, and murdering tens of millions, if not hundreds of millions, of innocent human beings, in the Gulag Archipelago; seems to be a major historic event, that requires far more attention and scrutiny, than it is now receiving. We grew up through the World War II celebrations of our parents' generation. The fall of the Berlin Wall, is our generation's major historic event, which we have lived through. It seems astonishing, that there is almost no discussion about the Gulag, and the current Chinese Gulag system, that is still executing dissidents. There is also a noticeable absence of concern, for the cathartic events, leading up to the fall of the Berlin Wall.

41

Some of us have been conditioned, to fall into a contrived obsequious stupor, at the mere mention of Auschwitz; but what percentage of the products, that we buy from Wal-Mart, are produced by doomed dissident inmates, who are being worked to death, in Chinese concentration camps? Where is the outcry from our labour unions, about the jobs that have been wiped out, by the flood of cheap products, which are destroying many manufacturing industries, and exacerbating an already staggering trade deficit? Where is the corresponding enthusiasm and moral concern, about the events surrounding the Cold War?

Environmental concern is reminiscent of one of Pierre Elliot Trudeau's old slogans: "Participatory Democracy". This phrase automatically implied that what had hitherto been practiced, before our messiah Trudeau came along, was lacking in some way. By the very way the environmental concern issue is introduced, we are already being accused of complicity with the polluters (big industry and the private sector), if we don't immediately submit to the environmentalist dogma. How can anyone possibly be against the sacred high and mighty environmentalist conviction?

Political activism and genuine concern are two different things. Environmentalists who suppress disagreement are simply not interested in pursuing the truth. These are ideological activists with a hidden agenda, who are using environmental concern as a straitjacket to muzzle dissenters. Leading climatologists from MIT and other prestigious universities have found that:

- Man-made carbon dioxide emissions are roughly five percent of the total annual carbon dioxide emissions produced by nature, by Volcanoes for example
- Oceans are responsible for most greenhouse gases
- the Sun's sunspot activity is probably a greater contributor to the rise in the Earth's temperature than any other factor
- Carbon dioxide levels are also a product of climate change, in contrast to environmentalist claims that the reverse is true.

The free market cannot solve anything by itself, but the free market can, by using incentive, allow creative people to solve all of our problems, as has been the case, throughout history, where the free flow of information was permitted and coercion curtailed.

Not all, but some environmentalists are creating a climate of fear, where those who question, are repeatedly shouted down and treated like lepers. When freedom of speech dies, freedom dies with it. I do have real concern for the environment, but that doesn't mean that the environmental movement hasn't been concocted by the left, who needed a new vehicle and constituency to pursue their radical socialist/economic agenda, after the ideology of communism suffered from the historical realities of the Gulag and it's own financial and moral bankruptcy.

Karl Marx, the inventor of modern day communism, originally coined the term Capitalist in his book "Das Kapital", a critique of free-market industrial society. Thereafter the term has been invoked by the enemies of free-market economics to refer to greedy selfish industrialists who "exploit the working class". Free-marketers like to call themselves conservative, libertarian or liberal. The system is called Free Market Economics, and was not invented by any one person but, has evolved over thousands of years of trial and error.

George Orwell started his political life as a celebrated socialist author, who regularly wrote social justice issue novels and newspaper articles in London, England. Orwell was so devout a socialist, that he even went to Spain to join the fight against General Franco and his FET y de las JONS. Luckily for him, Orwell was shot in the neck during the war and sent to hospital. This is how he managed to evade the executions of idealist socialists by the Soviet Army, who had entered the war during his recovery.

When he got back on his feet, he learned of the arrests and executions of some of his best friends, whom he knew to be true believers in socialist ideas. This is when he started to turn against the ideology of socialism and communism. He read many socialist writers like Rousseau and was inspired by Rousseau's analogy of beasts of burden on a farm compared to the working class in France's hierarchical monarchy, when Orwell himself wrote his satire of the Russian Revolution: "The Animal Farm".

Socialism is the centralization of economic decision making, into the hands of a single government "soviet" or council. All three opposition parties want to do this to different degrees. In Canada, the Greens and the NDP, who really would like to eliminate the whole idea of profit altogether, want to extend this soviet style control, to all aspects of the economy, as was practiced in the former communist Soviet Union. Both of these political parties also share a firm seminal foundation in a communist past. The Liberals, who also have a long sixteen year history of flirting with socialism, during the Trudeau years, want this to a lesser degree. Stéphane Dion promised not to tax profit but, only said he wanted to tax pollution. Bill Clinton ended all of his 1992 campaign speeches with the firm promise, not to raise taxes on anyone earning less than $200,000 a year. Of course, as soon as he was inaugurated, his administration proceeded to raise the taxes on everybody, 4 days afterward.

The Liberals were accusing the Conservatives of guilt by association, for the economic turmoil caused by the sub-prime mortgage scandal, in the United States and the ensuing instability of the world stock markets. As usual, socialists are using the trouble on Wall Street, as a false pretext, to repudiate free enterprise market economics, which is a different thing, entirely. Free market economics says that people should be allowed to set any price they want, for their services or products, without any government interference or coercion. There are, however, certain crimes, which even the staunchest free market proselyte would want the government to pursue, such as insider trading, fraud and embezzlement. The fact that the ham-strung American Congress fails to pursue these criminals, is not the fault of free market economic thinking but, rather special interest group lobbying or bribing, in which both American political parties share the blame, almost equally.

The Stock market never was the true economy, it is merely a tool used (and sometimes severely misused) by companies, to raise capital. In some instances, it has

45

become gambling on an astronomical scale, that leaves the door open to speculating sharks, to be able to destroy or crush perfectly good companies or banks, simply to make a huge cash-in or profit. Oliver Stone erroneously equated "Wall Street" with the "truest form of Capitalism", in his agitation propaganda picture "Wall Street". The original purpose of the stock market was to invent a way of protecting people who owned shipping companies from the vagaries of high risk, by inviting many other people to invest in their companies and become shareholders. This would more evenly distribute the losses but, also the profits, when they came. This technique was first practiced by the Dutch, who were sailing ships around the Cape of Good Hope, at the notoriously stormy southern tip of Africa, trying to transport black pepper back to Europe, from India and the Far East. Only two ships, out of three, made it safely back.

The value of the shares in a particular shipping company would rise or fall, depending on carrier pigeon news reports of the likelihood of one of its ships being able to make it safely around the cape. For instance, if there was bad news, then some investors would start selling their shares off but, if it turned out later, that the ship in question, had been spotted off the west coast of Africa, then the price of the shares would sky rocket! This, unfortunately also ushered in the inducement to gamble, by some more risk happy investors, who wanted to "rake in the money", as it were. So there is a dark side to this invention, which must be carefully understood and watched by the authorities but, it is not a reason to vote for socialists hiding behind the false ideologies represented by the red or green flags.

Nazis and other Socialists

The similarities between Hitler's National Socialists and Stalin's International Socialists are overwhelming. Both ideologies repudiated all religions and were atheistic, both regimes depended on the rule of command, as opposed to the rule of law. In both systems, private ownership was either curtailed or abolished and in both systems people who were considered dangerous because of their views or ethnicity, were executed on an industrial scale. Worker's unions behind the Iron Curtain were instruments of the party, and an insult to the actual workers, whose rights they were supposed to be protecting.

What about the workers unions in China? Why don't they demand better safety measures for coal miners? The savagery of communism is just as bad as anything Hitler could ever dream up. How was the quality of the Gulag any different from Auschwitz?

Documentaries and museums that show photography of the Third Reich, or pictures from inside the Nazi regime, usually are only shown in black and white, despite the fact that German engineers had developed color photography to a high degree, before Hitler had come to power. Nazi banners seen on all facades in the streets in the background, were predominantly, socialist red. Red is the color of socialism. Western socialists don't want people to realize that they had many affinities with the Nazis.

Socialism is based on three basic principles that both regimes shared; solidarity, obedience and chauvinism. The solidarity of sharing was cultivated by the Nazis, starting in the HJ or Hitler Jugend (Hitler Youth) where the children were routinely made to exchange lunches with

47

each other, to destroy any family preferences or special advantages. Group gymnastics and exercises were cultivated at all levels as a way to foster the feeling of being bound together, in a group. Hitler and Stalin both abolished true democracy and installed themselves as despotic tyrants. Conservative estimates say that Stalin's Gulag had exterminated 55 million innocent Russian people, during peace time.

These are compelling similarities that leftist zealots, cannot simply sweep under the rug, any more.

People's Car

Volkswagen literally translated means people's car, in German. In every aspect of life and society in Germany, during his tenure, Hitler cultivated socialist measures to guarantee a basic minimum safety net for the working man, including the ability to acquire a set of wheels! The Volkswagen, as we all know, is no Dodge Charger, it is an economical, sensible car for a family of four, which was designed with affordability as the first and foremost characteristic. Profit was not the motive. It was personally commissioned by Hitler of Ferdinand Porsche, the chief automobile designer, in Germany, at the time.

Hitler's socialist programs were pervasively spread and more thoroughly and successfully organized, probably, than in any other socialist country, in the world. The Volkswagen is just the most salient residual legacy of this ideology. Germany today boasts some of the most powerful social programs and unions in the world, and much of this is due to Hitler. Socialists just don't want it to be true.

Ideological Sustainability

Marxism is a political/economical philosophy named after the German thinker, Karl Marx who described it in his many writings, which were sometimes co-authored with Friedrich Engels back in 1844, before the appearance of the internal combustion engine, which was invented by Nicholas Otto, in Germany, in 1867. Marx put "the greater good" or "the collective" at center stage, while placing individual liberties, on the back burner.

The Marxist Utopia sounds good when you read the theory, in Karl Marx and Friedrich Engel's books because the intent was to create a fair distribution of wealth and to prevent the exploitation of the working class, by the elites of society. The wealth of the worker's production should also be equally shared, by the workers themselves and not partially stolen by the owners of industry. One of Marx's cardinal errors was to assume that products and services possessed an intrinsic monetary value that could somehow, by an act of measurement, be calculated. This axiom provided the foundation for the idea that prices and wages should be fixed, at some "fair" level, by the central committee or council, or "soviet" in Russian.

We are coming to the Green connection, in just a bit. The Bolsheviks decided to put Marxism into practice, in Russia, after the Russian Revolution, in 1917. Marx and Engels did provide the intellectual foundation for the revolution, and the Soviet idea was launched by the Bolsheviks, who were lead by Leon Trotsky, Vladimir Ilyich Lenin and Joseph Stalin. In Marxism there is a cap put on wages, so people who work harder are not given any more money. This is necessary, in order to make the fixing of price possible, which was one of the chief defining principles, however false, of this ideology. Human nature has a way of tending to relax, if people know that they will not benefit any more, by an increase in effort. You do the bare minimum that is expected of you, since any sustenance of additional stress will not be rewarded. When this tendency was multiplied across the whole population of a country the size of Russia, at the time, there was a profound stagnation, in the economy. Production levels went down.

This aspect of human nature was not foreseen by Karl Marx. This is the point at which the Utopia turns into a nightmare, the point where Marxism becomes Stalinism. It became clear to the revolutionaries, early on, that eventually they would have to use coercion, on the people, in order to force them to make sufficient efforts, and further, to lock the borders of their country, so that no one could simply leave and go to another country, which was not running along the ideas of Karl Marx. Communism, in other words, is Marxism applied. Communism is Marxism modified by the necessary incarceration and coercion needed to make Marxism sustainable. How did this coercion work? If someone was identified as having a lack of enthusiasm for their work, they could be labeled "dissident" which made them candidates for the concentration camps, in Siberia, known as the Gulag system. Here they would also have to work but, there was no pay and conditions were abysmal; if you got sick, there would be no medicine and no medical care.

Millions of people, some historians say around fifty-five million were worked to death, in these camps, over the stretch of time, from 1917 until 1989, when Communism finally collapsed. There were special camps

50

for dissidents who were considered to be particularly influential and therefore dangerous. These were the Uranium mines, where inmates were not provided with any protective gear and were intentionally exposed to the radiation from this mineral, in order to hasten their deaths. Dissidents were forced to work, even while they were dying of cancer. Marxism cannot exist in the real world, without force or coercion, and so Communism became it's expression.

Nazism and Communism are both forms of Socialism. One was Socialism with a nationalistic agenda, while the other one still pursues an international missionary theology. The fact that the Nazis were Socialists, is obfuscated in some books, exhibitions and documentaries by the use of black and white prints exclusively, although all 3rd Reich photography was produced, in full color, a proud new development of German technology. In 3rd Reich photographs, the color red dominates pervasively, due to the use of red banners, by the Nazis, who wanted to demonstrate their loyalty to Socialism and the working class. The German, Karl Marx wrote Das Kapital, which was a blueprint for the establishment of a Utopian society, based on egalitarian redistribution of wealth and hatred of the rich. The Austrian, Adolph Hitler wrote Mein Kampf, which was his blueprint for the establishment of a new society, based on the imperative of bringing everyone's *Weltanschauung* (world view) in line, with the intolerant dogma of the Aryan collective and the total rejection of liberal international capitalism.

It is a fallacy, however, to assume that the followers of Hitler or Marx, derived their energy from these literary doctrines, however intellectually appealing those doctrines might have seemed, at the time. The true source of the powerful emotional energy and motivation behind both ideologies, comes from one and the same place; it comes from deep inside our most primitive instincts, which have evolved in us, over the past four and a half million years. We have evolved into perfectly optimized hunter-gatherers. This is how we humans have lived for the vast majority of our history. Our modernized commercial world is only a very recent development, within which, we hunter-gatherers, have suddenly found ourselves, in an unfamiliar anti-septic world, of acoustic tile ceilings, high by-pass ratio turbo fans, bewildering financial structures, and beleaguered ethics, struggling to keep up, with scientific progress.

Socialism is an attempt to acquire conditions, in a society that feel right, once again, because we all hunger, deep down, for the simpler relationships, with the rules of the jungle and the familiar collective group, that we long to be part of. The rule of law, the division of labor and commercial organization that have accompanied our modern industrial society, while promoting freedom of thought, have separated many of us into isolated and lonely people. The free market system has produced businesses and economic modalities, which are far too complex, for the lay person to even begin to fathom, let alone understand or feel comfortable with. Bond markets, credit default swaps, derivatives, hedge funds, collateralized dept obligations; these are queer animals indeed, if you are not directly involved with the financial services industry.

This desire to re-acquire more satisfying environmental circumstances, is also the motivation of the flower children of the sixties, tree huggers and the

Environmental movement, who all, really want to turn the clock back, one million years, or so. It is all understandable. It is a desire to return to nature. Hitler's *Bund Deutcher Maedchen* (Alliance of German Girls) and HJ (*Hitler Jugend*) Hitler Youth, following his doctrine of total body and mind health, all had to practice gymnastics outside, in the fresh air, in order to grow up healthy Aryan milk mothers and soldiers, for the 3rd Reich. The sanctity of *Mutter Erde* or mother earth was one of Hitler's deepest held convictions, which was part of the mystical Aryan culture. He was a Boy Scout himself, and great admirer of wholesome mother earth. The FKK or *Freie Körper Kult* (Free Body Cult), in Germany, which is a nudist movement today, is a direct out-growth of these old Nazi environmental and mystical beliefs.

When Nikita Khrushchev allowed the book to be published, in the fifties, Heinrich Böll read "One Day in the Life of Ivan Denisovich" by Aleksandr Solzhenitsyn. Böll who was a well-known left-wing writer in West Germany, won the Nobel prize for literature in 1972, wrote many novels which championed the working class and criticized right-wing ideas in general, after the Second World War. Khrushchev, who represented a new hope for the world, when he declared Joseph Stalin a mass murderer, opened the gates of the Gulag, briefly, freeing Solzhenitsyn, for the first time. Böll, who still believed in Communism, could appreciate the evil of the Soviet Gulag and attributed it to Stalin. The true idealistic intentions of Khrushchev could not, however prevail, under the weight of the need to keep people incarcerated, in the Iron Curtain countries, which was most clearly visible around the Berlin Wall, that Khrushchev had given the order to build, in 1961, in direct

53

response to John F. Kennedy's woeful Bay of Pigs betrayal, in Cuba. Khrushchev also reassured by this Bay of Pigs failure, sent nuclear tipped inter-continental ballistic missiles to be deployed in Cuba, precipitating the famous Cuban Missile Crisis.

In 1973, when Aleksandr Solzhenitsyn was exiled by the Soviet Union – the KGB wanted to kill him but, didn't want to risk martyring him – Heinrich Böll took him in, and invited Solzhenitsyn to stay in his house, in West Germany until he could get himself settled. At this point Solzhenitsyn, gave Böll a copy of his new magnum opus "The Gulag Archipelago". Böll and his think tank of three younger radical students, Rudi Dutschke, Petra Kelly and Joseph Beuys, realized how morally bankrupt the Union of Soviet Socialist Republics really was, even beyond Stalin. Böll who must have been able to see the writing on the wall, in light of rhythmic Communist recidivism, knew that Socialists would have difficulty recruiting young people, in the future. Intellectuals in Western Europe took great interest in The Gulag Archipelago, and began to shun the ideology behind Communism and Socialism, in alarming numbers. A new packaging was needed for their left wing ideology. How could Karl Marx and Friedrich Engel's Communist Manifesto be made more palatable in light of these new revelations about the Gulag system of coercion, repression and mass murder, which even the idealistic Khrushchev, eventually had allowed to resume?

One day Böll's young think tank had a stroke of genius. Why not simply take every reference to "the worker" and "the working class" in the Communist Manifesto, and replace it with "the environment" and "nature"? Then the color red can be replaced with its complement, the color green and instead of calling it the Communist Manifesto, the name should be changed to the "Green Manifesto". This new constituency of trees and animals had the added advantage that they couldn't be interviewed. The bad guys didn't need any replacing, they are still the same capitalist "pigs", corporations and the military industrial complex. And so, the Green Movement was born, in West Germany in 1975 and later the first Green Party in the world, was established, also in West Germany, in 1979.

Of course there was always some interest in nature and mother earth, even in the Hitler movement of not too long ago. Monte Veritas in Switzerland in 1905 is probably the world's first hippie commune which was established by the kids of wealthy industrialists. They rebelled against the establishment, did drugs, let down their hair and danced in the nude, to poetry readings by such literary luminaries as Hermann Hesse, who was also a companion. This ecological/environmentalist strain lay at hand and does have some affinity with powerful hunter-gatherer socialist instincts, buried deep within us. Böll decided that this green substitution was the correct answer to the growing fear of Socialism, that the left wing desperately needed, to acquire a new image, with which to appeal to younger generations and persuade people, to "give the government control over the commanding heights of the economy", Vladimir Ilyich Lenin's famous battle cry. So the environmental movement is a kind of green Trojan horse, created by the left to replace the old socialist rhetoric, which has been largely discredited by the fall of the Berlin Wall and the collapse of the colossus of Soviet Communism, back in 1989.

The Green movement is like a watermelon, green on

the outside but, red on the inside. The main goal of environmentalism is to increase government regulations and restrictions in order to strangle the free market economy. According to the Green rhetoric, only the government bureaucracy can be trusted, to run big industries, which pose a potential hazard to the environment. So they want our economy to be centrally controlled, like in a communist system.

Chapter 3

The Liberation Agendas

The language of truth is plain;
it needs no cosmetics, while fraudulent talk,
inherently diseased,
needs craftily concocted medication.

Euripides, 413 B.C.

Girl Power

Most women are working because their husband isn't being paid enough? What about the legions of serenely indifferent, complacently supine and inimitably sovereign young career women, who have no husband and are out earning everyone else, not due to real merit, but because they are exploiting the demand that they find themselves in, sexually? Young women today, have the world by the tail, and they know it. They don't feel like victims.

Their biggest complaint is that in marriage one is condemned to having sex with the same person for the rest of one's life. These aren't victims who need to work, they are spoiled brats who can't ever get enough money to support their shopping habits, and for whom very few men could ever come close to being good enough. At five o'clock, these monarchs drop their mice and leave the office, because they "have to be somewhere". They don't worry about getting fired.

Try this if you're a man; try leaving early as often as these precious princesses, and see what happens. Men usually stay until the wee hours to make sure that presentation is ready for the next day. If they aren't willing to make that sacrifice, then they might get the boot.

When men were on top, they at least gave some thought to ethics and morals. It had been a long evolution of societal patterns and structures which had created the institutions of religion, law and family, which men generally tried to pay respect to, for everyone's sake. Men supporting jobless women was never an issue, it was considered normal. How many career women are willing to support a jobless man? The last thing the supine princesses of today care about is ethics. Sex and money are their sole concerns. They don't even care about feminism!

"How much does that loser have in his bank account? I wouldn't touch a man with a ten foot pole, unless he has six figures in his bank account." This is the sort of conversation young women are having with each other today. Swell.

Young women rule. "It's raining men". Young women have a major advantage over men, in the iniquitous love market. All men, between the ages of 18 and 90, want to be with the same iconic trophy wife, who is around twenty, slender and attractive. But despite their advanced years, only the wealthy Hugh Heffners or Donald Trumps can afford these delightful acquisitions. This means that for the rest of the young men, it's a tough squalid slog, which accounts for the relatively high incidence of crime, homosexuality, violence against women and suicide among younger men.

In our perfidious left wing media, tis the season to always portray women as the downtrodden. Men are the evil oppressors, who "make twice the money while working half as much as women". These histrionic myths are constantly being spun, by left wing politicians such as Bob Rae, former leader of the communist front party in Canada: the N.D.P.

Women are happier, as is evidenced by the statistics Canada fact that women live ten years longer than men, on average. Therefore, women are not as keen to even enter into politics, a profession basically for the ideologically or emotionally unsatisfied.

Some young men find it difficult to resign themselves to,

having to choose between being alone, homosexuality or the serene ultimatums, at the but end, of a modern girl's mercurial vanity. So these hot-heads go out, get a gun and mercilessly shoot as many young women as possible, in retribution, before, hopelessly taking their own lives. In the event of school shootings, the real issue is, of course, sex - not gun availability. Now, if you make it more difficult for people to acquire guns, is this going to prevent a determined suicidal avenger from getting one? Don't forget, there is always the black market.

The consequences and iniquities being caused by the girl power paradigm, need to be better understood, so that they can be appropriately redressed. Has feminism gone too far? Are we being punished by the invisible genocide of contraception and abortion? Are too many women abandoning their prerogative of starting a family, in deference to the materialistic pursuit of a career? Is it all the girls' fault or are other less obvious, exacerbating proclivities involved, such as pervasive adultery committed by powerful older men? Perhaps the Pope's position on contraception is not as dumb as the left wing, amoral media would have us believe? Perhaps ethics are important after all?

Guns were easier to get back in the fifties and sixties, when the entertainment on T.V. included such cowboy series as Bonanza, High Chaparral, Rawhide and Gunsmoke, which routinely illustrated the solving of problems by gunfire. John Wayne, the mascot of the Rifle Association, was the blockbuster hero of this era, and yet we didn't see any school shootings or severe crimes committed by twelve year olds, the way we see them today, in a time of androgynous values and political correctness.

Since guns were more available and there were no school shootings, therefore gun availability is not the problem.

The emergence of this school shooting trend must have another cause.

Feminists who observe the inimitable sovereignty of modern young women are quick to take the credit. By placing morality in abeyance we are tilting the playing field; giving an exaggerated advantage to young women and rich men, on the one hand, at the expense of an acute disadvantage to young men and older women, on the other hand.

Women generally have the luxury of being able to rely on a man for financial security, in addition to the newly won option of a career alternative. Men on the other hand, only have the one possibility of a career for security. Most women are not willing to support a "jobless loser", therefore, it is not merely a question of role reversal as the feminists claim, but rather one of role displacement with detrimental consequences not only to the men who have been replaced by women but also for society on the whole. Men without a future are a burden to society if they have to be supported, and a danger if they turn to crime.

Successful middle aged and older men are abandoning their wives at an alarming and increasing rate in order to marry more attractive younger women. Some older men even keep several mistresses suspended in the hope that each might be the lucky one who will be selected to be their new bride, although they usually have no knowledge of one another. These men are often in their sixties while their mistresses are usually in their twenties! Some young women, however, are more or less, stuck in a relationship with a married man thirty or so years older than she, not necessarily due to love, but often because they have had a child together and the older man will do anything to continue the relationship. In a startling number of cases, he will divorce his wife and marry the younger woman. After all, he is the professor, or the owner of the company. These men may not have much to offer as far as sensuality is concerned, but they are certainly in a position to shower their mistresses with gifts, favors and security. Younger men usually only have their youth and plans for the future to offer to these supine princesses, who are already intoxicated by the demand in which they find themselves; and, confronted with the question of whether to run the risk of a life of struggle with a young man, who might turn out to be a loser, or go with the sure thing, the older man who has already achieved something.

The population demographics of developed northern countries are tending toward a progressively older mean age on the Gaussian normal frequency curve. This means that the vast majority of the population is over fifty, and the number of young people is dwindling. If we extrapolate our princesses little dilemma onto the general population we begin to get a sinking feeling that this is not an unusual situation. Due to the fact that we have a negative birth rate (because of birth control and the decline of the family) the number of old people is ballooning way out of proportion. The relative supply of young people is shrinking dangerously. Under these circumstances, it doesn't take too many older men to effectively raid the supply of younger women.

People who are in love are much happier and more emotionally stable than people that are alone.

Consequently, young women tend to be satisfied and optimistic about their lives. Young men, on the other hand, are generally bewildered and in some cases hopelessly frustrated. This accounts for the increase in homosexuality, gang warfare and violent crime, particularly, crimes targeting already scarce young women. An incredible eighty percent of all suicides and all crimes are committed by young men in their twenties!

Feminists use the above fact to justify their claim that men are inherently more brutal and vicious than women. Young men are not more evil than women, they are less happy! And women entering the workforce are exacerbating the problem of availability because they have decided to take the career road, leaving themselves with even less time for relationships, unwittingly abating, if not entirely forfeiting, their potential to establish a healthy family.

One of the classical differences between the right and the left has been the question of whether behavior is inherited or conditioned by society, where the left was usually of the opinion that behavior is learned. Then there is the question of evil. The left doesn't want to accept this concept because the left is generally agnostic or atheistic and needs to be able to touch things, before it can be assured of their existence.

In the case of young boys shooting their classmates, I think we may be able to rule evil out, because these shooters often commit suicide after-wards, and do not gain any benefit from their murders. It is pure evil if a man rapes a six year old girl and subsequently strangles her, in order to evade identification. In order to acquire a moment of selfish pleasure and remain anonymous, the murderer takes

63

an innocent human life. People who commit suicide are driven by a belief or conviction, however misguided this conviction may be. They would argue that, it is the community around them that is evil, and who would hastily rejoin such a claim?

Perhaps these shooters are afflicted with some kind of mental illness caused by their parents' use of drugs, in earlier years, as has been cogently suggested by Waiting for God, or perhaps they are suffering from schizophrenia. But what if there are two shooters working as partners, and both seem to share the same convictions, apparently with equal enthusiasm, as in the case of the Columbine massacre? What are the chances that both individuals have inherited the same rare bug? Both shooters did, however, have career mothers, and fathers, neither of whom had the time to ask what they were interested in or what they were doing after school.

In the case of Mark Lepine, the shooter at the McGill University massacre of 15 young women, in Montreal, Canada, in the fall of 1989, he actually came out and identified feminism as his primary target. Why not take him at his word for this motive?

Twisted Sisters

Homosexuality and feminism are adopted siblings. Like siblings, they share many similarities but, they also have quite different characters. Feminism is a political movement that has a long established history of campaigns, while homosexuality, lacking any concept, is simply a reactive affliction with a history, mostly of being in the

64

closet. In recent times they have become political allies instrumental in setting standards.

The unremitting rhetoric of political correctness has prohibited all prudent speculation about the contributions and consequences of these psychotic ideologies. Both groups are made up of people who have great difficulty controlling their emotions, and who have, ironically, decided to shun the opposite sex. They both have pseudo justifications but, upon closer scrutiny, either one can be shown to be a fallacy by any intelligent ten year old. That is why they get protection from the politically correct movement, under labile constructs of cumbersome prevarication, which require continual maintenance.

When you strip homosexuality down to its basic reality, cutting through all the politically motivated orthodoxies, you are left with sodomy. The insertion, for mere stimulation, of the male reproductive organ into a partner's waste drain is filthy, unnatural, unhealthy and the essential defining act of this perversion. But, because of the sheer number of proselytes, gayness has gained cultural status. Some have adopted attitudes of superiority over other people, which are really quite unjustified.

Militant feminism is founded on the hatred of men. It is a fanatical form of chauvinism developed by women who have come to reject traditional examples of society, which they regard as instruments of repression and male supremacy. Originally, suffrage was earned as a privilege of citizenship by risking one's life on the battlefield. Women were discouraged from participating in combat to ensure the best chances for a society to procreate. Men had to be remunerated in a meaningful way, for bearing the full weight of the consequences of a community's decided policies. Feminists have created a false pretext around this voting issue, to be able to illustrate their fraudulent claim that men had always been oppressing women.

In every normal family, everyone knows who really runs the show; the hand that rocks the cradle. Career women who earn less than a million, risk forfeiting their chance at having a family of their own, if they wait too long to have children. It has been shown by many sociological studies undertaken in California and England involving hundreds of test families, that the children of working mothers are getting a raw deal, while the most well-adjusted and best academically performing children are from traditional nuclear families.

The danger is this; any large group of people united by a conviction or a cause, is a considerable constituency, and so, becomes interesting to politicians who want votes. By making overtures to these groups, in the form of supportive promises, politicians confer upon them an aura of legitimacy or respectability. If you find that society is being run by the touchiest members, then in a sense, that's twisted, because you're trying to take as the general standard, the standard of the people who have the greatest difficulty controlling their emotions in a particular area.

The Gay Delusion

To entertain seriously, the notions that the gay agenda is promoting, would be tantamount to engaging in a textbook exercise of Orwellian doublethink. It is symptomatic of our time's prevailing political correctness, to be expected to simultaneously, and without question, accept two diametrically opposed beliefs, in a single phrase - "gay marriage". Homosexuals who bother no one and, do what they do discretely, should be left alone. But disingenuous activists who attack our religions and institutions, should be assertively assailed; normal God fearing people have every right to defend their beliefs and traditional values.

Religion is an evolving guidance system of beliefs that only gradually adjusts to new insights and experiences along the way, only reluctantly, once they have been shown to be valid, which regularly accounts for friction, especially with more intelligent individuals. Some beliefs or related sets of beliefs eventually acquire the status of institutions, within this system. Marriage is such an institution and it is an essential component of every trusted religion, because it is the platform for the biological family, which in turn is the building block of society. In a religion, you must obey the rules. If you don't obey, then you run the risk of being ostracized; you forfeit your claim to membership by betraying some sacred principle.

Our civilization has a stake in promoting the conditions and values, which will support and strengthen the family unit, because family members have a better chance in life than orphans. The biological, nuclear family concept has proven itself over thousands of years of history, and is therefore, worthy of special discriminatory protection. Recent sociological studies undertaken in California and England, monitoring the lives of hundreds of test families, have shown that children of traditional husband and wife parents, whose mothers stayed at home, were most successful in school and most well-adjusted, emotionally.

Gay behavior is a perversion of sexuality as it was

originally intended by nature. The male reproductive organ was designed for procreation by an act of love between a man and a woman. Gays base their so called "alternative sexuality" on reciprocal masturbation. Homosexuality has no precept or edict. There is absolutely no theoretical foundation, biological necessity or seminal basis for it, and homosexuality has little to offer that could be considered, even remotely healthy. On the contrary, it has produced and distributed the largest and most deadly pandemic virus in human history: AIDS. Gay activists cannot win with real rhetorical substance, so they usually rely on sad testimonials -"you can easily get a partner"- and warn about "dangerous" stereotypes, such as Eddie Murphy's humor.

Homosexuality is a compensation for the girl power paradigm; an acute scarcity of eligible young women, due to the pervasive adultery, that is being committed by more powerful older men and especially due to feminism, which tells girls to pursue a career, instead of establishing a family. It is a form of behavioral disorder in most cases, but in the instance of sex change operations, severe psychosis. Lesbianism is another strange brew altogether, for one thing, curiously, there don't seem to be too many sex change operations! And gays out-number lesbians by about ten to one, roughly comparable to the ratio of young men to women in the available love market; just a coincidence?

On the one hand, proven traditional principles are to be shunned and are craftily allowed to be presented, in our media, by the religious right, in carefully edited rantings and ravings. We are supposed to divest ourselves of these outdated superstitions. On the other hand, against the backdrop of our conceited modern ethos, we are expected to exalt this perverse affliction lacking any concept, with sodomy as it's defining act, to the level of an alternative form of sexuality; a mercurial leap of pure faith. Is this the reward for our society's willingness to defend everyone's right to be different; that those who whine about tolerance, are busy trying to proselytize and coerce us into this false altruistic legislation, intended to destroy the family?

The Perverse Establishment

"We are sliding down into the mire of a democracy, which pollutes the morals of the citizens before it swallows up their liberties."

Fisher Ames

Timothy Leary, Hillary Clinton, Pierre Elliott Trudeau – these people and their ideological companions have created this new establishment, which sanctifies gay marriage, protects the criminal, promotes socialist values and generally is responsible for the deterioration of morality and traditional values, including the nuclear family. Feminism and emancipation theology have been a key ingredient in this toxic mix of political re-conditioning.

Our new politicians and political activists have orchestrated a massive campaign against the family that has been on-going for several decades. Compulsory mis-education in schools, attacking moral values by the application of Sex Education, feminism attacking family values, radical homosexuals vs. the family, the invisible holocaust of abortion politics vs. the family, and finally the re-writing of the definition of the family, into law. We are now to accept that homosexuals have the same rights as normal heterosexual partners in a Marriage. In our so-called democracy, we the people were not even consulted about this issue.

States who have wanted to control society, such as Communist East Germany, have tried to destroy the family unit, as leftists here have also been trying to do. Family members are more stable and secure in the world because they have each other to count on, in times of adversity. Orphans, on the other hand, are more dependent on government benefit programs. Healthy family members are more likely to grow up as independent adults, who rely less on the state for assistance, and therefore, political activists who put the state on a pedestal, want to destroy the family, so that there will be more foot loose dependents, who they will need for support.

Under this political and anti-moral onslaught, the fall-out has taken the form of, among other things, intense juvenile delinquency, such as the killing of classmates by young boys. Surprise, surprise. Women being brainwashed into pursuing careers has been a major pay-off, of this new theology, and a decisive and salient precondition to the harvesting of juvenile psychopaths. Young children need a mother at home for ethical guidance and emotional support. No day care worker is ever going to replace the biological mother.

War Against the Family

"Every human being, no matter where, on Earth, has one natural father and exactly one natural mother. These two individuals are responsible for and more likely than anyone else, to care about what happens to this child. This human triangle is a universal fact that is stamped on each and every one of us. This is the purest and most perfect "type" of family; the real thing. All other variations are less than perfect."

William D. Gairdner, The War Against The Family

The family unit represented by the union between a man and a woman, is the building block of a strong and healthy society because the children of this family have their parents and their siblings to lean on, in times of adversity. Blood is thicker than water. A large family with its accumulated wealth, in the form of land and businesses has proven, throughout history, to encourage independence for individuals and strength for society, on the whole. Healthy families do not require government programs for economic security.

Impoverished ghettos are usually populated by single mothers trying to raise their children and hold a job, at the same time. Orphans whose blood relatives are no longer in reach, for whatever reason, only have the state and government programs to rely on, for support, in times of distress. In all sociological studies, children of normal nuclear families, ie., with a mother and a father, have the best chances to develop into emotionally stable individuals who can become successes later in life. Children from single parent family units have the greatest obstacles thrown down in front of them, pulling them down into a life of dependence on welfare, or worse, a life of drug addiction and/or crime.

For the above reasons, our society, along with all societies based on religion, everywhere in the world, for that matter, has decided to extend special privileges to normal married couples, that is, heterosexual couples, who will be able to produce blood offspring, biologically. The

71

emotional bond between a child and it's biological parents is powerful. The emotional bond between siblings is also very powerful. That is why we have held these family units up for special protection through the sanctity of such institutions as marriage, in the church and special legal privileges, in society. The more people who can be encouraged to pursue these kinds of relationships, the better for all of society.

Leftists have tried but failed to remove those privileges from families, outside the Iron Curtain countries of the former East Bloc, led by the Soviet Union. Within these countries the traditional family unit was all but destroyed. Fathers were routinely ridiculed in television programs, in East Germany, for example, while the role of the new working woman was put on a pedestal. Feminism was pushed to the nth degree, in communist countries. Forcing women to work was a strategy, less of trying to empower women and more to destroy the family, by removing mothers from their children. Daycare centers were to take over the care for the children, and provide a forum for "political guidance".

Since communists haven't been able to take over in the West, yet, leftists have decided to use another strategy to attack the traditional family unit, here. If those privileges cannot be taken away, the same effect can be had by extending those privileges to everyone and gay unions, in particular, under the guise of "equality for all". If you grant privileges to everyone then, those privileges cease to be privileges, anymore. So it is the same thing as removing those privileges. The government in Canada, did just that, behind closed doors, without consulting the people, in the form of a referendum, in our so called "democracy". Our political activists on the left, are slowly killing our sacred family values off, piece by piece. And anyone who complains is denounced as a hate monger.

Feminism and Violence

The family has been under attack since the 1930's on this continent, and for longer, since the 1900's, in Europe. Feminism was one of the principle weapons used by the communists in East Germany and all other Soviet satellite countries, to try to destroy the family unit, once and for all. The family unit was seen as being one of the main obstacles to the proper development of a communist society. The party leaders thought that, if mothers didn't have time for their children, then the children would become available to government run, day-care centers that, could then play a more pro-active role in their psychological and political conditioning, yielding more pure and loyal communists for the future. So all women were required to work full-time, in all communist doomed economies. It is interesting to note, in this connection, that most leaders of communist regimes were sociopaths and mass murderers, and that their economies were all catastrophic failures.

Two unprecedented proclivities have been thrust precipitously upon us, one preceding the other by about twenty years. There has been a massive wave of women entering the work force in the seventies, and we have witnessed a new epidemic of serious offenses, such as the Columbine High-School massacre, committed by young boys, during the nineties. Is there a connection between these two trends?

Behavioral psychologists and sociologists have been studying family structures and children's environmental contingencies, for many decades now, in hopes of being able to identify causes of sociopathy, and other criminal determinants. Experiments have also been carried out with chimpanzees, deprived of their mother's touch, to help us understand anti-social behavior.

Women started to enter the workforce on a scale never seen before in history, around 1979, when Sigourney Weaver emerged as the sole survivor, in a fight to the death between humans and a formidable alien, in the sci-fi box office hit Alien. "You go girl!" is the refrain we've been hearing ever since. A decade later, we have witnessed an unprecedented disintegration of the family, all across North America. In the late nineties, the new symptom of twelve year old sociopaths killing their classmates, suddenly came upon us. We have also marked an increase in sexual predators, gang violence and homosexuality and the proliferation of the unprecedented AIDS pandemic, all over the world.

In these circumstances, is it unreasonable to question the validity of the assumption that the feminist agenda is a foregone conclusion? Children are effectively being denied access to their mother's attention, on an industrial scale. We may be harvesting sociopaths, and the first wave of a new bane, seems to have crashed on our shores already.

A gun can only kill if someone wishes it. It is the heart and mind of a shooter that control his body and command his finger to squeeze the trigger. That is why it is so important that children receive a balanced, emotionally stable upbringing in a healthy and loving family. For some gang members, the gang is their family! It is the only family they ever knew. A person's emotions can be like a powerful steed, that can easily bolt and run out of control.

Sociologists in England and California have studied large numbers of families over decades collecting data and monitoring their lives progress. In California, thirty nuclear families, or traditional mother and father parents with the father as bread winner, represented the control group. The second group also around thirty in number, had two parents, but they were both working. And the third group were single mothers. The two women sociologists doing the study, not only kept tabs on all the relevant data, they also became fairly close to all the people concerned, and were able to get a keen sense of how happy or unhappy people seemed to be.

The results were staggering. The children of traditional nuclear families were consistently, the most well-adjusted emotionally, and easily outperformed the other groups in their academic standing. Their mothers were always there for them when they needed support or guidance. The career parents' children didn't do so well; they seemed to have lots of emotional problems and their grades were lackluster in school. Some even acquired criminal records. But by far the most seriously challenged were the children of single mothers, who exhibited many emotional problems, drug habits, criminal behavior and they did the worst in school, many even having dropped out altogether.

When the problem children were interviewed, they painted a picture of loneliness, where there was no body waiting for them when they came home from school, and who watched T.V. and ate junk food instead of doing their homework. In some cases their mothers would put them on a drug program to help them cope with deep and prolonged states of depression, programs which usually led to serious drug dependencies, later on.

Chapter 4

Culture Wars

"Intelligence and learning are more easily
stamped out, than revived."
Tacitus, A.D. 98

Liberal Arts Education

Our western civilization is based upon the liberal studies of the Greek philosophers. Greek philosophy is unequaled by any other system of thought or belief system, because of the insistence on proof being sought for all hypotheses, finding the truth behind things and establishing a unified whole theory that shows how these truths are related to one another. Three basic subjects were identified and pursued systematically: Ethos, Logos and Eros, or: ethics, logic and aesthetics, in that order of importance. Today, we use the psychological euphemisms: motivation, learning and perception.

Thales (625 - 545 b.c.), known for the phrase "Know thyself.", was one of the first Greek philosophers and the discoverer of one of the most profound and important principles underlying science and technology, the "Thalean Circle" (see figure opposite). No other ancient civilization has been able to provide an all-embracing philosophical system as extensive and persuasive, nor has any other insisted on a clear separation of humanity from the animal kingdom. It was an axiom of Greek thinking, that Man or human beings, are on a much higher plane than animals. The three significant religions of Islam, Judaism and Christianity have also accepted this as a fundamental postulate. Other ancient civilizations like the Egyptian or Chinese, have searched for divinity in the animal kingdom, thus not making a major distinction between humanity and nature.

A major discovery of Thales of Milet illustrating his multi-facetted geniality

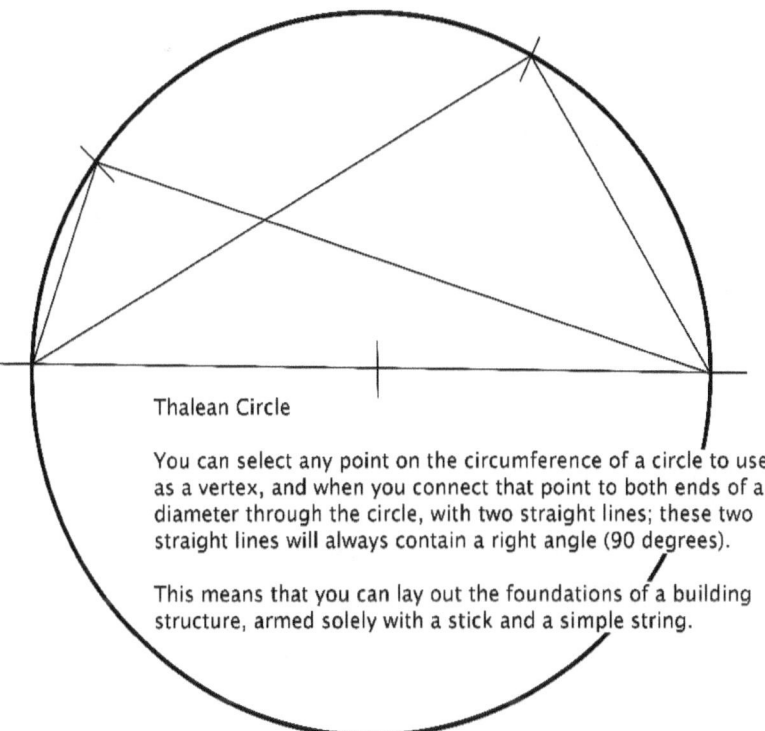

Thalean Circle

You can select any point on the circumference of a circle to use as a vertex, and when you connect that point to both ends of a diameter through the circle, with two straight lines; these two straight lines will always contain a right angle (90 degrees).

This means that you can lay out the foundations of a building structure, armed solely with a stick and a simple string.

The Relevance of Descriptive Geometry

"The artist who does not understand geometry, is like a captain who
sets sail on the open seas but, neglects to bring along a compass."

Leonardo Da Vinci

Descriptive geometry is the science of the legitimate or allowable imaging of three and more dimensional space on a flat plane. Drawings are the most important communication device for the architect, engineer and technician, whatever the medium of generation. If design or drawing can be thought of as a language, then descriptive geometry is the grammar of that language. One of the things which distinguishes human beings from animals, is our ability to use and recognize abstract symbols, such as characters of the alphabet, numbers, maps and plans. A writer doesn't necessarily have to be a master of grammar to be able to produce beautiful prose or poetry, but a thorough command of it will certainly give him a decisive advantage, over the unfocused pen-pusher.

Comprehensively understood, descriptive geometry has the means available, not only to present complex spatial relationships and situations correctly, but also to be able to solve peculiar tasks constructively, about these often seemingly impenetrable figures. Dandelin spheres, conic sections, axial affinity, the Rytz axis construction, the Thalean circle... these are just a small sample of the powerful tools, that enable a designer to succinctly target and pursue a clear solution to a specific design issue. In the absence or scarcity of such training, the designer, however talented, will be groping unscientifically, more or less, by trial and error, for a solution which will at best, produce a fragmentary satisfaction.

Precise intentions and their methodical parsing and execution, are the characteristic signature of a well organized professional who wastes little time, because he knows what he is doing, and why. All design disciplines in Europe, such as Aeronautical, Civil and Electrical Engineering, Architecture and Industrial Design invoke this science as a shared compulsory four year program of study, with some adjustments, at the universities; Kinematics, a subordinate study (planetary motion, dynamic systems, Wankel engine, etc.), compulsory for engineers, is offered to architects as an elective. For this and other reasons, European designers are the most intensively emulated and plagiarized in the world; this applies to all disciplines.

Finally, whereas technical drawing and model building in CAD programs are salient tactical skills, descriptive geometry is an intellectual asset that provides strategic understanding of the possibilities of organizing complex structures and their elements systematically, so that the desired intensions can be competently investigated and precisely met. CAD software provides a palette of primary tools and operations that can be combined to produce a wide variety of possible forms. To exploit this potential optimally, a knowledge of which solids to combine, what operations to perform, and in which sequence, is indispensable in order to be able to achieve the intended results.

All this is far beyond the reach of animals. Therefore, it is safe to say that not all human beings are animals, although some do behave like animals, from time to time. It wasn't the Christians who originally rejected the pagans. The emergence of the public square in Greece and Rome signaled the dawn of modern conceptual thinking, with it's recognition of the need for more complex interrelationships and their organization. This was a rebellious purpose because this space ex closes surrounding countryside, natural fields and the extensive amorphous space outside. This empty space was a thoroughly novel and intelligent achievement which separates human beings from animals and nature, especially nature.

Western civilization is a rebellion against nature; it always has been. It is the harnessing and restriction of our desires and instinctive motivations that enabled the development of the complex cities, some of us now seem to take for granted. Rules and regulations that tell us no, are what made progress possible; not simply following our feelings to where ever our fancies want to take us. Religion is such a harness. Just think of the Ten Commandments. They all begin with "Thou shalt not..."

Paganism vs. Religion

The definition of Pagan is a search for divinity in the animal kingdom. Ancient Greece was the beginning of Western civilization and the Greek philosophers decided to draw a line between animals and mankind. Before this, all other major civilizations, were pagan, because they worshiped animals as gods. We can see this in the hieroglyphs on the ancient Egyptian monuments. Animals don't have a sense of humor, they cannot count, they cannot draw with their claws or mandibles and they cannot understand abstract symbols such as the letters of an alphabet. They cannot think conceptually. "Modern" religions worship one God and He is above man.

As far as women are concerned, there is no male secret plan to exclude women from religious debate. Most people usually ignore religion, and it takes someone with extreme devotion to God, in any religion, to submit to the ways of the Creator, as delineated by all of the authors of these evolving religious systems. In times of trouble, people close ranks with their religions, as a kind of last resort. When these bad times happen, the priests, imams and rabbis are often in a dangerous position, because they will sometimes be targeted by the, usually male, perpetrators who are causing the trouble. Therefore, women are not encouraged to become priests, rabbis or imams. This is also the reason why priests in the Catholic faith are not permitted to be married, so that they have no family members that can be held hostage or tortured, to influence the way the priest behaves or whom he protects.

So it is not as an insult to women that women have been excluded from consideration as priests or, due to any insinuation that women don't measure up, intellectually. It is because an unmarried man, as shepherd of a flock of believers, has a better chance of survival against male aggressors, in a difficult social upheaval or calamity.

Western Culture

The World is trying to get into Western Europe and North America because the most desirable societies and the most successful economies are located in free democratic countries founded on Western culture. The first European colonies in North America, brought with them civil values

83

and traditions that enabled them to build up a resilient and powerful community. The native Indian groups, on the other hand, were migrants who's traditions were based on tribal hunter-gatherer precepts. European civilization is rooted in Greek philosophy, science and art and has evolved through thousands of years of optimized living in complex and highly organized cities. Euclid and Plato won out over the teachings of the Iroquois and the Inuit.

Greek philosophy is unequaled by any other system of thought or belief system, because of the insistence of proof being sought for all hypotheses, finding the truth behind things and establishing a unified whole concept that shows how these truths are related to one another. Two thousand three hundred years ago, Euclid discovered and proved geometrical theorems that still remain the basis for almost all of mathematics, science and technology today.

Other ancient civilizations have offered collections of wise aphorisms and produced impressive architectural monuments but, by and large, have continually sought divinity in nature, thus earning them the distinction of being pagan civilizations. Many current immigrants to North America are from third world pagan civilizations, who have very different values than the European based society, that has been created here, over the years. There is a danger that the very attributes that have attracted these newcomers, are under siege and in danger of extinction, if too many, too different are introduced too quickly, and this society doesn't have a chance to recover.

It must be emphasized that, if these people came here, then there must be a reason why they came here, and didn't chose to remain in their home countries. The sheer space available in North America is not the reason because

Europe is also a primary magnet. The most likely explanation is that this Western culture simply has more to offer than their own culture. Otherwise, we would be seeing "white" European Canadians emigrating to China, India, Africa or Central America. Western culture in North America has brought clear benefits, such as private property, freedom of religion, freedom of speech (currently in question due to hate crime legislation and political correctness), political freedom, the rule of law (as opposed to the rule of command of a tyrant), an extensive health care system, reasonably fair taxation, and a resilient economy that has been able to sustain a very large number of people, at a comparatively high standard of living.

The real question is: can people from Asia give up their values and learn to acquiesce in our Western values? Multiculturalism says that they needn't – and that is why it is a monstrosity. Pierre Elliot Trudeau invoked multiculturalism (massive immigration from the third world) in order to increase the constituency of the Liberal party, not because he cared about humanity. Motivated by hatred, he wanted to break the back of the English hegemony in Canada.

Perspective Distortion

Early settlers were small families who wanted to stake out a farm or ranch property of their own, so they could forge a life for themselves. The native Indians were hunter-gatherers who largely didn't have an organized agriculture to speak of. For food natives hunted buffalo, other animals, did some planting of corn crops, naturally occurring beans

85

and fished. In the beginning, the British didn't jump off their boats with guns blazing. There were good relations with natives because of this difference in culture and lifestyle and the fact that this continent was so large and had plenty of room for everyone.

In the beginning the number of European settlers was relatively small. Of course, as time passed, the number of immigrants from Europe, many of whom were deported undesirables, grew steadily and this eventually lead to some friction with the natives who must have seen this as a threat. The Europeans had the advantage that they placed value on a property, while the natives had a different understanding of the value of the land. The land belonged to no one and everyone, in their view. This is a basic difference in philosophy which was and still is at the heart of the struggle between natives and European immigrants. It is a totally different value system. I suggest, in as humble a way as I can that, people choose value systems which seem to offer more fruit or benefits, and this causes a process of evolution of political and economic ideas.

Older less promising ideas are gradually made extinct, just like in nature, when a particular species can no longer cope with the new conditions in a particular area. It is a fact that young native people also have recognized that there are obvious advantages to Western civilization, and they have embraced them, to their advantage. It was not solely violence which caused native culture to become side-lined. There is a natural process of selection by people, over time that determines which system of ideas will prevail.

Colonial Myths

Although there have been isolated incidents of massacres on both sides, there has never been a systematic extermination of native Indians, here in North America, that could be compared with the engineered famine, ordered by Joseph Stalin, in the Ukraine, in 1932, the mass murder of dissidents in the Gulag or the millions of ordinary people killed by Mao Tse Tung, during the "Great Leap Forward" policy of 1958 and the Cultural Revolution of 1968, in China. These deliberate mass murders are the biggest in recorded history, totaling on the order of, at least, one hundred million victims – no one knows the exact figure.

The above mentioned humanitarian atrocities have all been prosecuted by communist governments, during "peace time". This is how communists dealt with unfavorable demographics and constituencies; they simply had them killed outright or slowly worked them to death, in forced labor camps. Nothing of this scale, intensity, wantonness or intention can be attributed to any European colonizing power, anywhere in history. Allegations to this effect are either grossly misinformed or ill-intentioned.

Of course atrocities have been committed by the U.S. and the Canadian Armies on native Indians but, also by native Indians on European settlers. Both sides have been guilty of excessive hatred and fear mongering. Sometimes the truth is uninteresting and seems to lack drama. The truth of the native Indians is simply, that their culture couldn't compete with the vastly superior Western European culture. It doesn't have the urgency of genocide, or the moral conviction about the wrongness of stealing land from the ancestral peoples but, the truth is; Euclidean

Geometry won out, over Iroquois superstition. Native Indian culture simply couldn't offer any alternatives to European education, medicine, wealth, agriculture and technology.

The British have sustained colonies all over the planet, at one time or another. If they are so culpable for some of Africa's woes then, why did Hong Kong fare so well?

The West is the Best

If Asian cultures were really so good, then, why do so many people from China and India, flock to Europe and North America as eagerly as they do, for permanent residence? Is it because North America and Europe have more room? Or is it because we have a system that enables people to prosper and achieve more than if they stayed at home in comparatively poor India or murderous China?

If their economies and politics were fair and sustainable, they would remain in their home countries. But we see that people come to North America in large numbers, from these two countries in particular. People go where they believe they have more possibilities for a decent life. Western culture is superior, in politics and economics, and that is why they stream into North America. Hopefully the economies and politics in China and India do change for the better, not that they become Western but, that they leave their people alone and let them pursue their dreams.

People fleeing economic ruin, after decades of socialist experimentation, in their home countries of China and India, complaining about the "unfairness" of capitalism, in North America (as in the case of Olivia

Chow), is the epitome of hypocrisy. The precise reason these economic refugees made free-market North America their destination, is under attack by these stultified fortune seekers, pecking away, at the very branch on which they have landed.

It's not a racial thing, it's more political and economic. Pierre Elliott Trudeau's monster, Multiculturalism was invented to bolster support for the Left wing, then more at home in the Liberal party in Canada, than it seems to be today. It is not as kosher to be "Leftist" due to the collapse of the communist colossus, the Soviet Union and, the fact that communism and socialism have turned out to be such abysmal failures, in the twentieth century, throughout Africa, India and China.

Canada's 16 Year Experiment with Socialism

Canadians have been sold down the river because of the staggering debt that Pierre Elliot Trudeau, prime minister from 1968 to 1984, produced while he pursued run away tax and spending. Trudeau, the mascot of moral relativism and leftist cynicism, brought a weaker Canadian dollar; under his reign, we saw inflation soar to 16%, because he needed to print money like Slobodan Milosovic, to pay for all of his multiplying social engineering and egalitarian welfare programs, to say nothing of the millions that he funneled to his friends in Quebec. During his 16 year tenure, he raised taxes a staggering 938% from what they were in 1968, before he took office. To illustrate his communist desire to nationalize the economy, the number of crown corporations went from 38 in 1968, to 368, when he left office, in 1984. In 1968, Canada's dept was 58 billion dollars but, by 1984 it had risen to 378 billion dollars because of his "deficit financing". He was also the brain child behind Multiculturalism, a program to sharply increase immigration from the third world, in order to increase the Liberal constituency, and try to destroy the English/Conservative hegemony, in Canada, once and for all!

Reminiscent of the maniacal father character portrayed by Jack Nicholson in Stanley Kubric's "The Shining", Trudeau's eyes could not hide the cynical disdain he held for anything even remotely hinting of duty, honor or country. More finely in tune with the Flower Power ethos of Woodstock than with any concern for the economy or national security, it is easy to picture this mod "enfant terrible" shaking hands with Joseph Stalin and Mao Tse Tung at the Communist International or "Comintern" of 1952, in Moscow, where he clandestinely represented Canada, as a member of the NDP. In an interview he gave during the 1968 election campaign, he was musing over a blacklisting he had received from American customs (he had been barred from entering the United States):

"I presume the reasons for it to be twofold: I had been to the economic conference in Moscow in 1952, at the time Stalin was at the height of his power, and there were not many foreigners going to Russia (at that time)... and needless to say that I was wrongly attacked when I got back for being a Communist. That was probably one thing that helped. Another thing is probably that I had always received left periodicals and papers and I suspected then that there was some check on the mail, who is on the mailing list and so on. So, you know, they must have arrived at a conclusion that I was interested in ...

progressive things."

"Trudeau once on Blacklist", Ottawa
Globe and Mail, 1968, Geoffrey Stevens

Delegates invited to the annual Communist International or
Comintern, in the Soviet Union, were all, of course,
Communists. What would anyone who wasn't a Communist
be doing there, meeting Mao Tse Tung and Joseph Stalin?
The leaders and representatives of Communist parties from
all over the world attended this Comintern, members from
the Communist party of France, Italy, Germany, Austria
and from the Communist front party in Canada, the NDP, in
which Trudeau had started his political career.

No one in Canada would dare to defend Trudeau
during the election campaign of 1984, when the Canadian
electorate fiercely punished Trudeau's Liberals for the
immense damage they, and no one else, single-handedly did
to the economy, during their deliberate sixteen year
shakedown of Canadians' hard earned savings. The
Canadian people were fed up with Trudeau's blatant lies,
deception and vicious attacks against his dissenters and
mere critics, so they gave Brian Mulroney the biggest
landslide victory in the history of Canada, and left the poor
Liberals with 15 seats in the House of Commons, one more
seat than the NDP!

The value of the Canadian dollar was greater than
the US dollar, in 1968, before Pierre Elliot Trudeau, the
"messiah" was elected. By 1984, when Trudeau was finally
given the long overdue boot, it had dropped to half of its
original worth, vis a vis the US dollar.

Multicultural Downsides

The original intentions of multiculturalism were, ostensibly, to foster a spirit of trans-cultural cooperation, understanding and harmony, so that we could all live peacefully and productively together, in our multi-faceted communities. Obvious advantages of multiculturalism are a wide variety of culinary choices, art, philosophy, literature, music and dance. Pierre Elliott Trudeau was one of the architects of this multiculturalism but also had ulterior motives. Trudeau, who was from Quebec, originally, was a Francophone who, perhaps with some justification, hated the English hegemony, in Canada, due to the history of the English in Quebec. He also thought that, by bringing large numbers of immigrants in, from third world countries, with Soviet Marxist economies, such as India and China, he could guarantee a strong and lasting constituency, for the political Left.

Forty years on, we are witnessing some unpleasant realities, which have taken root. Unfortunately multiculturalism was administered, in an undifferentiated way, guided by the dubious edicts of politically correct prescription, which, among other things, presumed that all cultures are qualitatively equal. Trudeau also de-throned English as the only official language of Canada by, forcing French onto a predominantly English speaking Canada, to further disrupt the English hegemony. Official documents are printed in almost all third world country languages, at the Toronto City Hall, today. There are signs and pamphlets there in Swahili, Urdu, Hindi, Cantonese and a host of other nations tongues but, not German. There are some cultures, apparently, that are not good enough, for our politically correct bureaucrats. Perhaps it is hoped that Austrian, German and Swiss tourists will feel unwelcome, when they visit.

Some cultural groups, like the Chinese-Canadians are taking advantage of these latitudes by speaking Chinese with one another exclusively, enjoying the benefit of not being understood by their non-Chinese fellow Canadians. This has obvious merits in business negotiations but, it also is extremely selfish, rude and disruptive of that original goal of multiculturalism, namely understanding. Consequently, non-Chinese are made to feel extremely uncomfortable, in office situations, where Chinese is spoken by an enclave of exclusive people. It certainly doesn't promote a team spirit. Business owners and managers should insist that only English be spoken, for the benefit of all concerned.

If too many groups are pursuing their own self-centered issues, then the national social fabric will become so fragmented, as to threaten dissolution and ultimately, perhaps even civil war, as we have seen in the former Yugoslavia. There are now a plethora of selfish motivations that are encouraging this schizophrenia in our society. The Jews have the Holocaust campaign, the Chinese have their language, the Aboriginals have their persecution claims, the sub-continental Indians have their "culture", the Muslims have their intolerance of Liberalism and on it goes.

Almost every cultural or ethnic group has it's own favorite fears and paranoias, the indulgence in which, takes it further away from a friendly union with all other groups. By hammering away at everyone else, using one's own last resort, shot-gun clinching argument, we are exclosing each other and becoming more indifferent to other points of view. North America has become a collection of entrenched competing camps or lobbies. The misunderstood Chinese (who seem to be promoting that misunderstanding), the hurt Jews (yet rich and influential), the persecuted Aboriginals (who enjoy many special exceptions), oppressed Women (who enjoy sexual sovereignty), etc., etc. Chauvinism breeds racial and group contempt and the fragmentation is exacerbated. Multiculturalism has become a euphemism for chauvinism.

Heart of Darkness

Mao Tse Tuung was hand-picked by Joseph Stalin to establish communism in China. Mao revered Stalin and when Khrushchev denounced Joseph Stalin as a mass murderer, during the Communist International or "Comintern" in 1953, the year of Stalin's death, Mao got up, walked out and declared Khrushchev a stooge of the West. That was the beginning of the Sino-Soviet split.

In China today 68 offenses carry with them the death sentence. These crimes range from pornography distribution to tax evasion. According to Patricia Treble of Maclean's magazine, 10,000 people get the bullet in the back of the neck, every year.

The Dark Side of Multiculturalism

Pierre Elliott Trudeau invented multiculturalism as a tool to dilute our Western culture and increase the constituency of the Left wing. He was a disgruntled Francophone who wanted to break the back of the English hegemony in

Canada and favored immigration from third world countries like India, because people from such places were more likely to vote socialist than immigrants from Western European countries.

It is not surprising that people who grew up under socialism find it difficult to thrive in a free-market economic system and, demand that it be made more "fair". The trouble is that as we become more fair or "socially sustainable" our economy will gradually sink into poverty itself and North America will resemble these third world countries more and more, not just in terms of it's new visible majorities but also in terms of irreversible and endemic poverty and squalor.

Christianity is the foundation of our Western civilization, and has been for over 2,000 years. As such, it is target number one, for the Marxists. Western culture brought the world organized free market trade and commerce, medicine, mathematics, science, technology, sophisticated music, architecture and theater – a wealthy and enduring way of life capable of sustaining millions of people at a relatively high standard of living. Our Christian faith, in the West teaches us, in different ways, that we have a soul, that we need to work on, so that it will survive the death of our body. If you do not work on your soul, it will expire, when your body dies.

"The concepts of mercy and forgiveness are absent from Hinduism. In Hinduism, men do not pray to God for forgiveness, and a man's sins are never forgiven- indeed, there is no one out there to do the forgiving. In your next life you may be born someone higher up the caste scale, but in this life, there is no hope. For Gandhi, a true Hindu, did not believe in man's immortal soul. He believed with every ounce of his being in

95

karma, a series, perhaps a long series, of reincarnations, and at the end, with great good fortune: mukti, liberation from suffering and the necessity of rebirth, nothingness. Gandhi once wrote to Tolstoy (of all people) that reincarnation explained reasonably the many mysteries of life. So if Hindus today still treat an Untouchable as barely human, this is thought to be perfectly right and fitting because of his actions in earlier lives. As can be seen, Hinduism, by it's very theology, with it's sacred triad of karma, reincarnation, and caste (with caste an absolutely indispensable part of the system) offers the most complacent justification of inhumanity of any of the world's great religious faiths."

Richard Grenier, Capturing The Culture

Live 8 Agitation Propaganda

The G8 countries were being asked to forgive the dept of African countries, and send more money as so called "Live 8 (Aid)" in 2005. An appeal is under way, directly aimed at individuals of the developed nations to help put pressure, on their own governments, to send tax-payers money to people in need, in Africa. Bob Geldof, a "Boom Town Rats" pop music group has-been, and Bono were promoting this campaign.

There are 53 countries in Africa, 14 of which are democratic and, more or less, free. The 39 remaining countries are Marxist inspired, tyrannical regimes, which are engaged in persecution operations against dissidents that vary in intensity, from ethnic cleansing to civil war. Ethiopia, Nigeria, Liberia, Ivory Coast (was democratic until recently), Democratic Republic of Congo, Angola,

Algeria, Chad, Sudan, Senegal, Somalia, Kenya (also formerly democratic) and Burundi are all embroiled in civil war, where at <u>least</u> one thousand civilians are being killed each year, in each country!

In the quieter Zimbabwe, where Robert Mugabe has been in power for forty years or so, a government connivance had been sustained, with gangs of thugs who went around murdering and terrorizing white farm owners, during the late nineties. The agricultural industry of Zimbabwe was once the envy of Africa; today the industry is in ruins, and the people are hungry. The murdering thugs who wanted the land, didn't have any constructive skills, and continue killing anyone suspected of having been loyal to the "capitalist pigs". Mugabe imprisoned his opposition, and has started a campaign of bulldozing houses, orphanages, hospitals and schools down, that are located in areas, where there are larger groups of opposition constituents.

The agenda that is in effect in these corrupt dictatorships, is called "The Politics of Exclusion" by natives. The leaders and their cronies are enriching themselves at the expense of everyone else. A similar procedure was practiced by Slobodan Milosovich in the former Yugoslavia, also a site of pervasive ethnic cleansing and Marxist inspired ideology. These regimes used to get support from the Soviet Union during the cold war, but now support has been cut off. The problems in Africa are not due to acts of God, they are man-made, and quite deliberate.

In 1984, there was a famine looming in Ethiopia,

which inspired wide spread generosity around the globe. Two Canadian freighters were filled with milk powder, grain, rice and other essential materials and food and sent to Ethiopia, in an effort to save the people from starvation. A few days later, when the ships were off the coast of Ethiopia, in the Red Sea, their captains received a cynical greeting. They were told that if they wanted to berth their ships at harbor, they would have to pay $50,000.00 each, in harbor tax! The astonished captains protested, that this was a humanitarian mission, and not a commercial venture. The harbor officials repeated the serene ultimatum.

Bob Geldof and Bono are false prophets, and intellectual criminals, feigning piety and moral sovereignty, while, in reality, obfuscating deliberate humanitarian atrocities and, aiding and abetting their perpetrators - with the help of our money and negligence. According to his rhetoric, the reason why people in Africa are poor and starving, and dying of AIDS, is because we, in the developed countries, are selfish and rich! The real reason for their plight is that they are slaves to their governments, and the murderers who run them. Sending more money to these countries, with no strings attached, will have the effect of increasing the size of these despots' Swiss bank accounts, but it won't change anything for those who are being persecuted. Monetary aid must be linked to political reforms on the ground, and ways to monitor and guarantee that those reforms are really working.

Seventeen trillion dollars have been sent to sub-Saharan Africa between 1985 and 2005. Since then, twice as many people are living below the poverty line. Most of the money has been confiscated by corrupt leaders and their bureaucrat cronies.

Private property, the rule of law, as opposed to the rule of command (of a tyrant), and political and religious freedom are the four principle reasons for our countries' financial wealth and success. There are a lot of old socialist diehards out there, who won't accept this simple truth, and who continue to try to intimidate us with their political correctness. The twentieth century has witnessed the spread of socialism and it's consequent extermination of hundreds of millions of people in Russia and China under the rule of Joseph Stalin and Mao Tse Tung, Stalin's protégé. Now, the residue of socialism is still trying to cling to power in China, North Korea, Cuba and Africa.

Notes

Chapter 5

The Church Of The Devil

"Whom God intends to destroy,
He first deprives of his sanity."
Euripides, c. 425 B.C.

Hollywood Deception and Illusion

"You will never find a more wretched
hive of scum and villainy"
Obe Wan Kenobe, Star Wars

Film has the ability to bewilder us because it employs two
powerful media simultaneously; light and sound. Of these
two, sound is the more powerful and primal influence,
although some people don't realize this inconspicuous fact.
The art and science of film-making has evolved into a
highly sophisticated array of disciplines, which has as it's
goal, to convince the audience that, it is not film at all but,
reality. This is an open deception because some movie-
goers know that what they are watching is make-believe.
Deception is central to the whole enterprise of suspending
disbelief, as can be seen, in the special effects department.
    Stanley Kubrick pioneered the way space ship
models should be filmed, when he had a rather large and
intricate model made of the Jupiter mission ship. He needed
a way to make his leviathan glide forward smoothly, across
the silver screen, without revealing any means of structural
support, in his 1968 epic 2001: A Space Odyssey. His
genial trick was to put the much smaller and of course,
completely invisible camera, on a dolly track mounting and
move it backwards, instead! George Lucas was so
impressed by this scene, in Kubrick's film, that he used a
similar sequence to open his own blockbuster sci-fi epic
Star Wars, in 1977, where he pulled a camera backwards
slowly, on a track, using an electric motor, first under
Princess Leia's Blockade Runner and then finally, under the
much larger belly of an Imperial Battle Cruiser, supposedly

in pursuit. Ridley Scott then followed suit, when he let the seemingly massive Nostromo space freighter glide serenely, into view, in his smash hit, Alien, in 1979.

One of the most salient duties of a deception technique, is to go utterly unnoticed, as in the case of the beautiful arts of Matte painting and film editing, which are old, reliable but, invisible canons of film illusion. George Lucas also made extensive use of the lesser known technique of Matte painting, in his Star Wars film series. Matte painting is an acrylic and air-brush painting usually done on a sheet of glass, leaving an opening, through which actors can be filmed performing a particular scene. This painting must, of course, have the correct perspective, in order to look absolutely realistic, so that the audience will think that it is real. This is how the Death Star's cavernous Shuttle Bay was created, in the memorable arrival scene of Darth Vader. The only thing that was real was the access ramp of Vader's shuttle and the storm troopers, in the foreground. The arrays of storm troopers, in the background, were painted in, as was the structure of the bay itself. Today the computer has become heavily involved, in the image processing of this matte painting art, as well.

Unfortunately some people are completely deceived by film and regard it as the truth, in many instances. Many people don't read books. The mass media like television, is a delicate rhetorical tower built upon the foundations of ideas developed in books. Most political pundits and viewers are doing battle around the spires of these towers, while more sophisticated political rhetoricians look deeper at the foundations of the arguments, to find the flaws and cracks which underpin or, indeed, undermine those lofty towers. The deeper one goes the more obvious it becomes that, conservatives have the better arguments, history and experience on their side. But this can only be seen in books. You won't find too many real conservatives on mainstream television or on the big silver screen.

The Left knows that most people don't read books, so they have struggled early on, to capture the popular entertainment culture, through the mass media of movies and television. Sergei Eisenstein, who started out his film career, when sound was not yet part of the art, pioneered the political propaganda film, after the Russian Revolution, in 1917. He was a master of visual film editing, who developed the process of Montage, which is a powerful way to compress narrative time, into a short but dramatically effective set of images, juxtaposed to evoke an intense emotional reaction, in the viewer. His Soviet propaganda was overt and sanctioned by Joseph Stalin. Leni Riefenstahl's films, such as Triumph of the Will, in 1934, were also of an overt Nazi propaganda nature, perhaps inspired, to some extent by Eisenstein but, it was Hitler's shrewd propaganda minister, Joseph Goebbels, who taught the Left that the best propaganda should be so well disguised that, no one even suspects that they are viewing propaganda. The spectator is supposed to believe that he or she is merely watching a love story or an adventure. The ideas and symbols are to be subtly embedded in the dialog, with the utmost of care.

Melodic intonation conditioning is a powerful device that is used in movies and television to create a composition of melodic elements with image elements, which is a more sophisticated form of film editing, than conventional Montage, which merely juxtaposed image elements. Melodic intonation is a key motivational signal, to the spectator, of the meaning of the entire theme in a movie, or documentary. It is absolutely critical to how the audience is supposed to draw an inference, about the moral value of the material which is being presented. The very same piece of film can convey, in the mind, of the viewer, two diametrically opposed emotional casts or potential meanings, depending on this powerful musical effect. If we consider a scene of a van driving along a city street, depending on what kind of music accompanies the scene, various completely different expectations can be aroused, in the audience. If the music is up-lifting and happy, then we might imagine that the driver is off to some cheerful occasion, but if the music accompanying this scene is discordant and atonal, we suspect that the driver is, up to no good.

 In addition to it's pictorial or graphic attractiveness and musical pleasure, the mass media of movies and television, which was first developed by the Germans, who broadcast the 1936 Olympic Games, in Berlin, to bars equipped with futuristic television sets, in all the major cities of Germany, also has the power to sustain public opinion, a veritable belief ethos or "Zeitgeist" that needs much effort, to cultivate and maintain. The Italian Marxist Antonio Gramsci, whose famous battle cry, during Benito Mussolini's reign was: "capture the culture", thought that those who want to change society must change man's consciousness, and that in order to accomplish this they must first control the institutions by which that consciousness is formed: schools, universities, churches and, perhaps above all, art and the communications industry.

 One celebrated Gramsci disciple, Rudi Dutschke,

the late German student leader and later co-founder of the Green Party of Germany, formulated the doctrine of "the long march through the institutions" which meant taking over the universities, arts, media and government agencies. This was one of the most radical leftists in Germany, back in the late sixties, displaying Marxist ideology, before his clever "greening" which would come later, during the seventies. Socialists and Communists in America, have been trying to pursue a similar strategy, from their starting point, in Hollywood.

The list of subtle Hollywood propaganda films is staggering: The Birdman of Alcatraz, Dog Day Afternoon, The Sting, Butch Cassidy and the Sundance Kid, Silence of the Lambs, The Gangs of New York, Goodfellas, Reds, All the President's Men, The Front, The Big Chill, Natural Born Killers, Daniel, The Last Emperor, The Way We Were, Running on Empty, Casualties of War, The Russia House, The Manchurian Candidate, The Verdict and Glengary Glen Ross, to mention just a small fraction. In these films, traitors, robbers and murderers are glorified and presented as chic, while innocent businesses or institutions are presented as evil and corrupt. Most of these films are well crafted, entertaining and were nominated for the Academy Awards, particularly the Sting, in an attempt to lend them additional respectability and credibility.

It seemed to be alright, to be a Communist, in America, during the roaring and tumultuous 1920s and 1930's. The Great Depression was believed to have been caused by Capitalists with bowler hats, who exploited the smaller investors, on the stock market, which had crashed, in 1929. The Socialists in the Soviet Union, who had won the Russian Revolution, after the First World War, in 1917,

106

seemed to be on the verge of producing a truly Utopian worker's classless society. Many people in America, joined the Communist party, in those days. The 1930s was also the time when Dr. Arnold Deutsch, host of the Communist Cell in Cambridge University, in England, successfully recruited and became the early controller, of the Magnificent Five graduates: Donald Maclean, Guy Burgess, Anthony Blunt, John Cairncross and especially Kim Philby, who would later become head of SIS, the British counter-intelligence service, all clandestinely operating, for the KGB. Warren Beatty's Reds paints a fairly accurate, if incomplete picture of these times. He neglected, of course, to show the brutal treatment and extermination of millions of people, who were opposed to Communism, in Russia. Due to the revelations about the extent of Communist infiltration, into the government of the United States, described in Whittaker Chambers' book Witness, finally, a lid was put on the Communist writers and directors in Hollywood, during the so called "Red Scare" of the 1950's. Communist friendly writers and directors had to learn to keep a low profile, and use metaphors and allegories, to illustrate their political beliefs.

As a subtle and sophisticated kind of retaliation, many left-leaning producers and directors have decided to ignore the threat of Communism altogether, as if it never even existed, at all. They are still pursuing this tactic. The scare Joe McCarthy put in them, fifty years ago, still smarts, today. Currently, Hollywood produces movies about every topic, under the sun, except Communism. This is particularly noticeable since, after a forty year Cold War, we have recently witnessed the spectacular collapse of Communism, back in 1989. One would think that there was enough material there, for at least a couple of blockbusters! But no, all we get are movies based on adolescent comic book heroes and, of course, the never ending story of World War II. This expedient serves as a convenient vehicle to continually intimidate voters, to stay away from Conservatism, since, it is implied that, Hitler was just a little further along, on the right end of the ideological continuum.

When Hollywood seems to defer to re-makes, it is as though they have run out of ideas. There have probably been ten re-makes of the Titanic story, where roughly 1,000 people died, for instance, implying that this was the worst maritime tragedy, in history. Yet, there is so much unexplored material in recent momentous history, not the least of which is the deliberate sinking of the Gustaf, the Stoiben and the Goya, by Soviet submarines, at the end of the war, in 1945, off the coast of Danzig, in the Baltic Sea. These ships were filled with wounded soldiers and women and children, trying to get to the West part of Germany, which was occupied by English and American troops. 20,000 women and children, mostly young women, were drowned, in these attacks. We, the West, won the Cold War, with a little help from the United States. The stress of mutually assured destruction seems to have, at least for a time, evaporated. The collapse of Communism and the fall of the Berlin Wall are major events of our lives, still etched in our living memory. Why are these events being ignored by Hollywood, which bombards us with a relentless train of inane and vulgar garbage?

Spiderman, Superman, the Transformers, King Kong, Indiana Jones, The Pirates of the Caribbean, Saving Private Ryan, Band of Brothers, Inglorious Basterds ; we are either stuck in a World War II time warp or, we get comic book re-makes served up, on the altar of the silver screen. Everything under the sun, *except* events leading up to the fall of the Berlin Wall. Most adolescent photo-realistic CGI (Computer Generated Imaging) blockbusters suffer from too much gratuitous hallucination and not enough concomitant logical narrative traction, leaving them with all of the rhetorical persuasiveness of a mushy Saturday morning cartoon. What is wrong with this fantasy? It fills young minds with a lot of confusing delusions and distracts their attention from salient problems and events that have truly happened or which are actually unfolding, in the real world.

The United States and the West won the Cold War, after forty years of intense political chess with the Soviet Union and it's massive military arsenal – a major victory for us that has been systematically ignored by Hollywood. Why? The dark secret is that some celebrities like the actor Richard Dreyfuss, don't seem to care what happened to millions of Russians, who were slaughtered in the Gulag, many of them Jewish, by the way but, they expect Gentiles to fall, into a contrived obsequious stupor, at the mere mention of Auschwitz. Dreyfuss wanted Hollywood to revoke the Lifetime Achievement Award, which it had given to Elia Kazan, because Kazan, patriotically revealed the identity of real Communists, operating in Hollywood, during the Red Scare. Communists were, throughout the Cold War and still are, declared enemies of all forms of religion, the West and America in particular. Communists committed untold numbers of humanitarian atrocities, before, during and after the Second World War, in Eastern Europe, Russia, China, where they still continue, and Asia.

Why should someone effectively uncovering these enemies, be accused of "witch hunting"?

Although there are many people who are genuinely concerned about what happened to *all* victims of the Second World War, the Holocaust campaign is being abused, by some, to coerce potential critics of their agenda, into reticence. The pretext for propagating this campaign so relentlessly, has been that people shouldn't be allowed to forget what happened, lest a similar fate befall another group of people again, in the future. But the reality is that, in this campaign, there is little to no focus, on similar crimes committed against Gentiles.

"In 1995 the US Holocaust Council, acting at Israel's behest, practically eliminated mention of the Armenians in the Washington Holocaust Memorial Museum, and Jewish lobbyists in Congress blocked a day of remembrance for the Armenian genocide."

Norman Finkelstein, The Holocaust Industry

This seemingly chauvinistic concern, fixated on a seven year period of Nazi history in Poland, ignores the industrial scale mass murders that have been committed by Joseph Stalin, Mao Tse Tung and Pol Pot. The assumption is that the Jewish mass murder, in Poland is a "prime" mass murder, while all other mass murders are "sub-prime", hence the special label. The real purpose of the Holocaust campaign seems to be, to condition Gentile acquiescence in a political paradigm, in order to acquire control of the agenda, in the court of public opinion and immunity from criticism.

110

"Critics run the risk of being labeled "anti-semitic" by a compliant and credulous press, conditioned and prepped to give banner headlines to any Holocaust-related incident, however preposterous".

Norman Finkelstein, The Holocaust Industry

Our media, in most Western countries, seems obsessed, with the Holocaust alone, and this creates the impression that the only people who committed mass murder, were the Nazis. We know, from the archives of the political police of the former Soviet Union and East Germany, that around 55 million people were murdered, in the Gulag death camps, between 1917 and 1989, and that, between five and nine million people, were deliberately starved, by Joseph Stalin, in the Ukraine, in 1933, *before* the outbreak of World War II. All innocent victims of mass murder deserve equal status in our memory. Socialism was the cause of these crimes against humanity, whether of the national, or of the international persuasion.

When the topic of the Cold War did come up, as in the movies, Dr. Strangelove, The Manchurian Candidate or The Front, the subject was cast in an ideologically ambiguous light and dealt with in a cynical way, suggesting that America's involvement was ill-considered, at best and misguided fascist reactionary patriotism, at worst. Soviet Communism and American Free Market Enterprise were cast as opposing twins, with equivalent degrees of culpability and confusion of purpose, like two dumb boxers, throwing punches at each other, for no apparent reason, implying that there is a lack of intelligence and symmetry of ethical or moral fault. The notion was that it didn't matter which system you belonged to; they were

111

essentially, interchangeable. This did not, however, square with the obvious fact that people, in Communist countries were incarcerated and had to risk death, if they tried to escape, while there were no restrictions on movement for us, in the West. The horrendous iniquities committed, by the left wing, under Communism, are not to be mentioned or referenced, in any way.

The Spy Who Came In From The Cold, 1965

Few people still believe in the moral symmetry between the former coercive, totalitarian Soviet Union and the free, incentive-driven democracies of the West. The great ideological contest, which we know as the Cold War, was finally won by us, in the West. Large segments of the media, which took a stake in promoting the notion that the West was just as bad, as the Communist East Bloc, now simply don't talk about it, anymore. But the old films and books they invested in, are still around, residue of the quaint misguided assumptions that were the foundation of our strangely obsequious Cold War culture, here in the West.

One of the architects of this ethos was David Cornwell, or as you might better know him, John Le Carré. He was the anti-Ian Fleming. Le Carré's spy characters were ordinary men and women locked in their own irreconcilable ideological posturing, trapped like flies in aspic, victims of their own rhetoric. At least, that is how he put it. Communist film directors and producers, such as Martin Ritt and Sydney Lumet, eagerly grabbed the opportunity to film Le Carré's novels owing to their

112

skepticism towards the West and their intricately nuanced, labile equivocating calculus, with respect to the ethical aspects, of the covert conflict.

Smug leftist pundits like to report that Cornwell or Le Carré, was an "intelligence officer" working on Her Majesty's Secret Service, just like Ian Fleming, the inventor of James Bond. When he was 19 and studying languages at Oxford, David Cornwell merely infiltrated far-left student groups and informed on them, to MI-5. He wasn't a paid employee of the Service. These activities came to an abrupt halt in 1954, when his father was arrested for fraud, jailed and couldn't pay for David's education anymore. In 1958 Cornwell was able to get a job at MI-5 as a translator and ultimately he was drafted by MI-6 and sent to Bonn, West Germany because of his knowledge of German. He quit the service, in 1963, when his novel "The Spy Who Came In From The Cold", became a run-away financial success.

Reading his novels or watching their film versions, it is obvious that Le Carré never saw the inside, of an Iron Curtain country. He wasn't an agent of the James Bond or Kim Philby caliber. He was merely a language technician specializing in German, restricted to translation desk duties. He never shows us the anguish of the inmates of these giant prison camps, pretending to be republics of the people. Feigning pragmatic ideological maturity, Alec Leamas, Le Carré's protagonist, induced into hearty laughter at the realization, that his gentle and stylish lover Nan, actually believes in Communism, buys himself a license to repudiate everything under the sun, including Father Christmas, God , Karl Marx and last but not least, Western political rhetoric.

113

The most contrived scene, in the Spy Who Came In From the Cold, is the secret trial to determine the loyalty of Hans-Dieter Mundt, an Abteilung assassin, relying on Leamas' testimony. This is the crown of Le Carré's over-strained intellectual ping-pong conjecture. In a Communist regime, such as East Germany, a captured English agent suspected of having knowledge of an operative's guilt, would simply have been tortured and interrogated to death. They would never require his personal testimony, in a trial, secret or otherwise. Leamas' character represents the Western forces of "good" but, he discovers that he has been used by MI6 and evil triumphs, when he is shot, on the Eastern side of the Berlin Wall. This is Le Carré's simple strategy: pretend to represent the West then, spit on it.

This was a standard approach employed by most communist Hollywood directors, in the post-McCarthy era, of fearless pride and American patriotism. In the less sophisticated movie, "The Manchurian Candidate", John Frankenheimer invests heavily in circumscribing the startling extent of Communist infiltration in high places, a fact fresh in the minds of audiences who had recently learned of Whittaker Chambers revelations about Alger Hiss, a KGB agent, in Franklin Delano Roosevelt's White House, a notion that also seems to be hinted at, in the title, itself. In this ostensibly, anti-Communist movie with a patriotic message, the son of a Republican dynasty is captured, in Korea and brainwashed into becoming a mole or sleeper agent, who has been programed to assassinate a presidential candidate, a plot which, as it turns out, in the surprise ending, was in reality orchestrated, by his own Republican zealot mother,... of course!

The meat and potatoes of Hollywood films, however, is to make money by entertaining but, at the same time, provide a vehicle or pretext with which to ridicule some idea based on traditional values. Subversive activists are glorified, while righteous enforcers of the law, are vilified. In case you think that a shortage of information about Communism, in entertainment blockbusters, does not prove the existence of a political bias favoring the left, in Hollywood, consider that Roberto Benigni, an Italian comedian/actor won an Oscar for his work in Life is Beautiful, in 1997, a film about life in a Nazi concentration camp, during World War II. Benigni was, and probably still is, a passionate activist Communist, who was filmed hosting a Communist rally, in Italy, during the 1980s, on stage, against a backdrop of large red Communist banners, complete with hammer and sickle, where he enthusiastically reassured the delegates that the candidate was a "true, one hundred percent Communist!" This news reel was aired, in Italy, France and Germany, shortly after Benigni won the Oscar, in Los Angeles. Now, had someone found out that Benigni was a Neo-Nazi who was master of ceremonies at a Neo-Nazi rally, what do you think his chances would have been, of winning an Oscar, in Hollywood?

The cold war crucible formed at least two diametrically opposed perspectives of what we, here in western countries, wanted to aspire to. The year 1969 was a climax of emotions and decisive events which defined the people, who found themselves, given the choice, between two major ideological philosophies. On the one hand, representing the hope, for an exciting future of modernity, we had engineers who were busy putting men on the Moon

115

– the Right Stuff camp; and on the other hand, representing a reluctance to embrace technology, we had the radical students who threw Molotov cocktails at the police, as they rioted on university campuses, and demonstrated against the Vietnam War, super-sonic flight and nuclear energy– the counter-culture camp, or the Consciousness Movement (1961-1975).

The Sixties bore some resemblance to the 1920s, which was also an era of social tumult and change, modern music and tension between the people and government, during the Prohibition. The Sixties Consciousness Movement however, was made up of, no less than, six major cultural revolutions; the Civil Rights Revolution led by Malcolm X and Dr. Martin Luther King, the Feminist Revolution led by Gloria Steinem, the Vietnam War Protests led by Jerry Rubin and Abbot Howard "Abbie" Hoffman, the Sexual Revolution led by Hugh Hefner, the Drug Revolution led by Timothy Leary and last but not least, the Green Movement led by Heinrich Böll, in West Germany. It is interesting to note that the leaders of all these revolutions, were not baby-boomers at all, who provided the energy and large support but, members of the previous Silent generation, who were born during the 1920s. Their young formative years, growing up, would have fallen, in the wake of the Great Depression, when Communism might have seemed to be, a preferable alternative.

Six, so intensely focused revolutions, all sharing precisely the same decade, don't happen in a society, as diverse as the United States, by pure coincidence; there must have been some intentional planning and coordination going on, behind the scenes. Hollywood luminaries, their

116

films and documentaries, and KGB resident controllers and their operatives, located in every major city, on the North American continent, played key roles in the cultivation, organization and dissemination of all of these revolutions. Rock and Roll was used by the counter-culture camp to co-opt and proselytize young recruits and help justify their aggressive agenda of "peace and equality", and distract attention from the geo-political Communist threat. This rock music became a pervasive soundtrack that gave a rebellious melodic intonation, to the whole period of the sixties and seventies. You had to acquiesce in this "flower-power" ethos, if you wanted to be "in", or free from intellectual brutality (name-calling or gratuitously accusing someone of being a bigot, racist or a fascist pig, etc.), in school, on campus and even at the office. In Canada, the first wave baby-boomers loved Pierre Elliott Trudeau, also a member of the prevenient Silent generation, who was banned from entering the U. S., before he was elected Prime Minister and seemed to symbolize the Woodstock spirit, for the younger baby-boomers. Although he was much older (Trudeau attended the 1952 annual Communist International or Comintern, in Moscow, hosted by Joseph Stalin, as a 35 year old Socialist delegate from Canada), he used trendy dress and his famous cynical tongue-in-cheek humor, to advertise his membership.

In ideological terms, the race to the Moon was a competition between the United States of America and the Union of Soviet Socialist Republics, from the point of view of the U.S., to deny the Communists the prospect of acquiring a lofty weapons platform, over the Earth. The hippie movement, acquiescing with the Communist agenda, to some degree, was a sheer denial of the Cold War, in

117

particular, and traditional values, in general. The world seemed to be going wild as hippies let their hair grow long and started to live in communes, along the motto, "turn on, tune in and drop out", brilliantly caricatured in the science-fiction epic Planet of the Apes. 1969 was also the year that the United States succeeded in this race, beating the Soviet Union and landing a man safely, on the Moon; Neil Armstrong. Around this time, the anti-establishment plays Hair and Jesus Christ, Superstar opened on Broadway, while the forward-looking Stanley Kubrick picture 2001: A Space Odyssey, featured quarreling Apes for the first half hour, before the breath-taking jump to the future, to Johann Strauss' Viennese Blue Danube waltz. The second wave baby-boomers, born between 1955 and 1965, were generally more impressed by the Kubrick vision of the future, and some shuddered at the sight of the older generation attacking policemen, getting high on drugs and burning computers.

Amid the clamor of the Sixties uprising, wrinkling the fabric of our traditional values, was hypocritical Feminism, which paid lip service to equality, while relieving women of the hippie imperative of rejecting the material world. So while young people of this age, were being told that the consumption of material goods was un-cool, young women were encouraged to passively-aggressively, follow the money. Girls would be re-programmed, in schools run almost exclusively by women teachers now, to reject the traditional pursuit of establishing and cultivating a family, in deference to pursuing a career, taking jobs away from men. Men were cast, as evil oppressors of women, who didn't even let women vote, in previous centuries. Feminism never provided an answer for

118

the hypocrisy that women will only marry a wealthier man, despite their new-found independence. Career women have also created the new phenomenon of the latch-key children, who have no one to come home to, after school, and can do whatever they like, in loneliness. The killings at Columbine High School are a recent example of this startling new legacy, of the feminist blight. Feminism dealt the most destructive blow against the most important institution of all, the family.

In 1973 Heinrich Böll moved away from socialism, as the pretext for the anti-establishment agenda and deferred over to environmentalism, when he read his friend's book "The Gulag Archipelago". Aleksandr Solzhenitsyn destroyed the benevolent myth of Socialism, as he described the true coercive nature of it's ultimate conclusion and the humanitarian atrocities of the Union of Soviet Socialist Republics, the Gulag death camps of the Soviet Union, which thankfully collapsed, with the fall of the Berlin Wall, in 1989. Böll and three other radical left-wing students, who started out as socialists in Germany, established the first Green party, in the world, in 1975, giving a new facade to the agenda of the left-wing, which has always been, to give the government control, over the commanding heights of the economy.

Today, the aging hippie Woodstock camp or first wave baby-boomers, like Al Gore, represent a new angle warning us about "Global Warming", telling us to punish the "Polluters" by hitting them with higher taxes. The sacrosanct environment is today's leftist panacea that we must all kowtow before. After having soundly lost the cold war argument, the strategy of the left has been simply, to change the subject of the conversation. His Hollywood friends helped Al Gore produce his CGI re-make of the 1969, The Limits to Growth agitation propaganda film, under the new title: An Inconvenient Truth, in 2006.

JFK, 1991

A solution to a problem or mystery does not only elude us, due to a lack of evidence, or lack of explanations, it sometimes does so precisely because of a cornucopia of explanations, points of view and theories. When there is too much explanation, that is when things tend to take on a mystical nature. Despite our advanced technological capabilities, some scientists claim that we don't know what to do with the nuclear waste, from our nuclear power plants. Area 51 is a source of stupefaction due to the many rumors about strange activities there, not because of a lack of UFO sightings or tall tales. Similarly, the assassination of John F. Kennedy has become a mysterious enigma, due to a flood of explanations and accusations, throughout history, since 1963. Oliver Stone has produced an amusing whodunit by pouring even more gasoline, on the fire.

Stone's entertaining movie JFK made in 1991, envelopes the audience in a smorgasbord of food for thought, distraction and delightful humor but, it doesn't make a convincing case to support his paranoid delusions about the evil, wicked, mean and nasty C.I.A. The hinge of Stone's argument, in which he invests so heavily, is the notion that Lee Harvey Oswald only had 5.6 seconds to get his shots off, which Stone also limits to three. Stone further infuses the film with a colorful cornucopia of conjecture and assumption, upon conjecture – all unproven or

120

unsupported by any real facts.

Indeed, facts are Oliver Stone's main adversaries, in this virtual universe of left-wing biased subjectivity. How does Stone back up his assertion that Oswald only had 5.6 seconds to kill Kennedy? Stone inserts the phrase "This is established by the Zapruder film" two or three times, in the film, at key dramatic focal points. That's it. No more detail or circumspection is offered to the audience to substantiate this central "clinching argument". The problem with Abraham Zapruder's film is that it was made with a 1960s 8mm camera and, it had *no* sound! This is an ultra-low resolution, high wow and flutter, silent home movie. There is no way this flimsy piece of evidence can establish very much, beyond the fact that the sun was shining and that the presidential motorcade of Cadillacs was moving, along the street.

Impartial objectivity is the first casualty in this movie, which is almost painfully obvious, to the audience, as Jim Garrison, a government bureaucrat and district attorney in New Orleans, is portrayed as the "good guy" by the much better looking Kevin Costner. Arguably the worst president in the history of the United States of America, John F. Kennedy is put on a pedestal in this three hour subservient hagiographic saga. Stone even includes the line "Never forget the death of your king", in Costner's tear-jerking closing argument. Not one iota of criticism is allowed to creep in, in any form, not only of J.F.K. but also not of Robert Kennedy, his nepotistically appointed Attorney General brother, nor of Martin Luther King, who are also cast as saintly martyrs. This is pure political propaganda, not necessarily of the most compelling kind. It really tries to be compelling but, this is one area where

121

Stone was trying too hard.

The reality is that there is no consensus and so many valid techniques, in the scientific community, as to how we should deal with nuclear waste, that opponents to nuclear energy have been able to exploit this, to erroneously conclude that there is no solution to this seeming conundrum. Area 51 is merely a proving ground for experimental top secret aircraft, which by definition, can be considered Unidentified Flying Objects. If we acquiesce in Oliver Stone's contention that there was something wrong with Earl Warren's investigations surrounding Kennedy's assassination, for the sake of argument, then we would have to look into all other possible theories and explanations for the shooting of Robert Kennedy and Oswald himself. There have been many theories proclaimed by different camps, to explain the Kennedy assassinations. One well known idea was that the Mafia was behind the killings as a pay-back to the old Joe Kennedy, the father of John and Robert, in keeping with well-established mob behavior, where rather than attacking their target directly, they sometimes hurt their target by killing the target's offspring or someone else, who is important to the target of their hatred. Another theory which lies at hand, is the possibility that Lee Harvey Oswald really was working for the KGB, who wanted to punish Kennedy for the embarrassment he put the Soviets through, on the world stage, during the Cuban missile crisis. Stone goes to great lengths to discredit this latter theory, by setting up the situation to make Oswald into a sort of double agent for the C.I.A. or at the very least, a fall-guy for the real perpetrators.

In a rare gesture toward a glimmer of objectivity,

Stone did include a scene where two of Garrison's deputies fall into an intense disagreement with him, resulting in the departure of both from Garrison's campaign. Bill Broussard, played by Michael Rooker objects to Garrison's obsession that the government assassinated Kennedy, in a coup d'etat, a la Julius Caesar, after Garrison suggests that the plot even went as high up as Lyndon B. Johnson, Kennedy's Vice President, who "was waiting in the wings". Broussard correctly points out that such a massive conspiracy couldn't have a chance of being covered up. Somebody would have come forward by now.

Oliver Stone is a conspiracy theory engineer who has become an expert at reverse engineering stupefaction. Generate confusion and stupefy your audience enough, then pour your fait accompli explanation down their eager throats. In the movie JFK, we are taken for a wild joy ride through several sub-plots which are all entertaining but, which only serve to further confuse the issue. Kevin Costner's character's children are always squeaking in the irrelevant background, whenever he is trying to justify his obsession with JFK, to his placid wife and we are treated to an endless train of impressions and red herrings, throughout the first two hours of the film.

In one, Jim Garrison acquires advice about this conspiracy from a retired director of covert operations calling himself "X", whom he meets in Washington D. C., in a Deep Throat style encounter. Garrison now plays the incredulous realist listening to a cynical informant, who overwhelms his naive victim with bewildering epiphanies about the grown-up realities of money, politics, power and the military industrial complex. Donald Sutherland gives a polished Hollywood performance which could have

123

otherwise, easily been interpreted as a disgruntled employee, who twists his own ineptitude into a story about how his former employers, needed to get rid of him because he would have been able to protect Kennedy. The actual unscripted meeting, if there really was one, would probably have been closer to two old losers on the Mall in D. C., convening to verify each other's self-importance, weaving a cumbersome conspiracy theory as a last desperate attempt at mutual commiseration.

"It's a mystery hiding in a riddle, wrapped in an enigma" is the refrain from a frightened Dave Ferrie, intensely played by Joe Pesci. Dave is paranoid and believes that "they" are after him and will soon kill him, shortly before his body is found, ostensibly having committed suicide. Of course this only strengthens Garrison's convictions about a wide spread conspiracy that will take America to a state of Fascism. In reality America has moved in the opposite direction, in the intervening years, witness the six cultural revolutions that have moved us all down the feminist, homosexual, environmentalist left-leaning politically correct ethos, and all of it's consequences, that we now have to cope with.

Aside from it's overt attempt to be "political" the film is delightfully entertaining, largely due to the wonderful performances by so many excellent actors, such as Gary Oldman, John Candy, Joe Pesci, Tommy Lee Jones, Kevin Bacon, and the list goes on and on. It is really fun to watch Tommy Lee Jones play Clay Shaw, a smug witty and enigmatic spook, who seems to be untouchable, despite his many flamingly eccentric vices. JFK is however a true piece of pure left-wing political propaganda. One of the most unfortunate aspects of this film is the long drawn out ending, where Costner whines about how fascism has returned to America. Costner's rambling run-on soliloquy is unbearably boring and ridiculous. When we hope that he will finally shut up, he starts crying and lamenting about all the children who were sent to fight in Vietnam. Garrison never gave this closing statement in the actual trial, this is pure Oliver Stone invention and opinion.

Good looking and charming actors are used to represent criminals, portraying them as heroes struggling in a world of chaos, against the cruel machinations of the rich elites, of the ruling class. The audience is supposed to develop sympathy for these outsiders of society, because they can't help the circumstances that they have relentlessly fallen victim to. There seems to be no other way out, except to lie, cheat, rob, kill, and rape, to make it, in our free and open western society, whose police are portrayed by over-weight sadistic bribe-takers, who we are supposed to despise. In Silence of the Lambs, directed by Jonathan Demme and starring Academy Award winner, Anthony Hopkins, a serial killer is even put on a pedestal, as a poet and artist, and nascent predators are exalted, invited and coached to feel free to kidnap, rape, torture and kill young women.

Dog Day Afternoon, 1975

In Dog Day Afternoon, Sidney Lumet explores the subjective point of view of the perpetrators of a major felony or violent crime, a bank robbery which turned into a hostage taking incident, that actually took place in New York, in 1972 and uses it to furnish Al Pacino, with a stage set to showcase his stand-up comedy/cabaret talents. The script is designed to get laughs from the movie audience and portray the armed robbers, as cuddly misfits, who couldn't hurt a fly and who are, more or less, drawn into these circumstances, by the pressures of our cold and indifferent society.

The protagonist of the story is Sonny, the leader of the gang, played by Al Pacino, a homosexual who ostensibly hilariously, needs the money for his lover's sex change operation, who, in turn, feels that he is "a woman trapped in a man's body". This line got the biggest laughs, from the movie going audiences, in the mid-1970s. In fact the whole script is really a series of one-liners that evoke laughter throughout the whole film, up to the shockingly serious ending, which is not funny at all, when the evil FBI finally put a cruel end, to this enjoyable party.

The police and law enforcement are portrayed as over-weight incompetent party-poopers, by such luminaries as Charles Durning, also the over-weight corrupt cop, in the Sting, who the audience watching the movie, as well as the audience behind the police barricades, are conditioned to ridicule, as this circus side-show develops. The bank facade becomes the stage for Al Pacino to make fun of the police, chanting political phrases of defiance, which gets the street crowd cheering for Al Pacino, and sets the viewers up, for Pacino's emotional "Attica" chant, which also got big laughs, from the movie audiences.

The "Establishment" is the bad guy and the robbers are the good guys, who are suddenly and horrifically dealt with, in the surprise ending, which seems to be designed to illustrate the cruelty of our law enforcement community. In reality of course, a hostage taking incident is a terrifying experience that no one enjoys, and armed bank robberies are usually extremely violent crimes. This reality is trivialized and the victims are shown to be on Al Pacino's side, in several instances, which also get hearty laughter responses from the movie audience. Although the film is very well crafted, and entertaining, it is a profound piece of subversive propaganda, coming from a director who, at least, didn't even deny that he was a passionate Communist.

Missing, 1982

It has become safe to say that if an American movie bears the etiquette "political thriller" this means that, it is in reality a Left Wing propaganda film. Missing, a film, which was directed by Constantine Costa Gavras in 1982, starring Jack Lemmon and Sissy Spacek is a persuasive case in point, although Costa-Gavras is a Greek born French movie director.

We get a patriotic middle aged American businessman's station point on the 1973 Right Wing coup in Chile and how he and his daughter-in-law are desperately searching for his son, an "idealistic" journalist, who went missing there. At first Jack Lemmon's character, Ed Horman suspects that his son and his daughter-in-law, played by Sissy Spacek, were involved in something or that his son did something to provoke his arrest but, as the movie unfolds, he becomes more and more suspicious of the American ambassador and his staff.

What is really missing in this so called political thriller, is a global overview that would show what the Right Wing coup was fighting against. Instead, we are intermittently exposed to scenes of political repression by the new regime, of the people of this South American country, as if to say that, the Right wing got up one day, and just decided to start killing people, for no apparent reason. There is also no information about what kind of articles Ed's son wrote, or what kind of newspaper he was writing for, only that it was considered to be Left Wing by the regime. There is absolutely no mention of the word Communist, from one end of the movie to the other, as if Communist terrorists and extremists did not even exist, in this part of the world.

John F. Kennedy opened the door to Communist infiltration, in Central and South America, when he decided to renege on promised air support to the Cuban expatriates, who tried to invade Cuba, in 1961 in order to take their country back, from the Marxist tyrant Fidel Castro. This and his further deal with the Soviet Union to not plan an invasion of Cuba, in exchange for the withdrawal of the ICBMs by the Soviet Union from Cuba, provided the Communists with a permanent "aircraft carrier" on the island of Cuba, from which to stage incursions into Central and South America, throughout the Cold War.

All The President's Men, 1976

A masterpiece of political propaganda and the mother of all conspiracy theories, which was almost immediately made into a two hour negative attack ad, against the Republican Party by the Left operating in Hollywood, in the middle of the Cold War was, of course, the book All The President's Men by Bob Woodward and Carl Bernstein. In this left-wing political thriller, a jagged mountain is constructed, out of a gentle molehill. The actual purpose of this desperate Washington Post exercise was to assassinate a right-wing president's character, and hopefully bring him down, the reality of which is twisted into innocuous investigative journalism, in the film version of the book. The esoteric elements of the Left hated the anti-Communist Richard M. Nixon, because of his role in bringing Whittaker Chambers' revelations about Communist infiltration into Franklin Delano Roosevelt's White House to light. Chambers' book Witness, which was published in 1952, when Nixon became Vice President, ultimately lead to the famous Red Scare, in the mid-1950s.

Daniel Ellsberg illegally leaked top secret Pentagon documents to the New York Times, in 1970, who in turn, illegally published them, in order to try to stoke resistance to the Vietnam War, in the court of public opinion. The so called "Watergate Scandal" was in reality, a media storm in a tea cup. If you strip away all the political hype, generated by the left-wing cheerleaders, in the media, you are left with an illegal but arguably justifiable entry, into the Democratic Party headquarters at the Watergate Hotel in Washington D.C., and Daniel Ellsberg's psychiatrist's office in California, in August of 1971. CIA agents, known as the "Plumbers" were looking for evidence against Daniel Ellsberg, who had perfidiously released the Pentagon Papers, an act of high treason, during President Nixon's first term. No one was hurt or killed, in this affair, which later turned into a feeding frenzy by the same left leaning American media that illegally published Ellsberg's Pentagon papers and hypocritical political theater, by the monotonous televised Senate Watergate Committee

Hearings, cast to resemble the Nuremberg Trials. While all this was happening, in 1975, Pol Pot was busy murdering millions of innocent people, in the rice fields, in Cambodia which was known to many reporters, who either chose to remain silent about it, or were ignored by their employers, because they didn't want to show that Khmer rouge Marxism needed to use mass-murder, in order to keep it's captive population under constant repression.

This whole Watergate incident is another proof for the left-wing bias and double standard, within the news and entertainment industry, in the United States, which is still alive and well, to this day. Nixon was doing the right thing, focusing on Vietnam and Cambodia, where the real crimes against humanity were actually unfolding, while the left-wing media only wanted to ignore this major story and concentrate on destroying a president, who had different political views than they had. What more proof does anyone need that the media puts their political agenda, before their desire to inform the public of real danger? All of this is of course not even mentioned, in the movie "All The President's Men", which premiered in 1976 and used the good looking actors Robert Redford and Dustin Hoffman, to portray the not so good looking Washington Post reporters Bob Woodward and Carl Bernstein. Credit must be given to the director Alan J. Pakula, for taking a pretty uneventful and boring story, and turning it into a suspenseful and entertaining piece of film making, even if the truth is only half-told and the suspense is the candy coating, for this pill.

The most salient scene in the movie comes near the end, to help provide the film with some semblance of a conclusion, when Redford's character, Woodward goes to meet Hal Holbrook's character, "Deep Throat", in a menacingly dark parking garage. Here Deep Throat whispers the core conspiracy and that "Your lives are in danger" to a stupefied Woodward, who hadn't even come close to realizing the incredible complexity of involvement and culpability of the whole American intelligence community, in this cover-up. If the intelligence community and the Nixon administration were really so deep, dark and dangerous, as the film suggests then, why couldn't they break into a hotel and a psychiatrist's office, without getting caught and sent to prison? What do we learn from all this? That the President and the intelligence community were involved in gathering information and engaging in clandestine activities. Oh, how shocking! If this is really a surprise to you then, you might be horrified to learn that there was never any Deep Throat and that there may not even be a Santa Clause! This avatar Deep Throat was most likely an invention of Woodward's, to be able to deflect accusations of inaccuracy, away from himself, if he wanted to field a conjecture, which he couldn't verify with any real facts. This kind of thing is even demonstrated quite clearly, on several occasions in the film, when Woodward and Bernstein pretend to know something, when they are interviewing someone, in order to acquire a confirmation, from this unsuspecting victim of their confidence trickery, in a surprisingly candid display of their true journalistic style.

The music is the real star of this movie. Melodic intonation is really key to how the audience is supposed to feel about people who worked for President Nixon. This movie is all about suspense, atmosphere and emotion, not about historical facts or accuracy, though it feigns to be objective and professional, by the use of an academically disciplined corporate looking introductory credits design and theme music which is almost militaristic and patriotic, in character. The theme music is reminiscent of a somber military funeral march, which sounds like it is being performed by a Marine Corps band. This is done to effectively obscure any hint of subversive intent. It takes on a mystical and foreboding aspect whenever Woodward and Bernstein may be on to something, such as in the Library of Congress, shot from the dome above, where the lens gradually zooms out, as a lower frequency heartbeat pummel delicately kicks in and gradually becomes louder and louder. We see more and more of the articulated concentric pattern, of the library floor furniture, which presumably is supposed to symbolize the reporters' growing perspective on Nixon's alleged ineffable web of intrigues.

This splendid example of political propaganda was also the political opposite of movies like The Green Berets (1968), starring John Wayne or The Killing Fields (1984), starring Sam Waterston, which wanted to warn the public, in the world and draw people's attention to the atrocities, which were being committed in Vietnam, at the hands of Communists and Marxists. The recurring theme in our media is that our intelligence community, FBI, the CIA and police are the bad guys, while investigative reporters are the good guys, who really care about our well-being. All The President's Men was an important installment in the ethos of Western society, which creates a conditioning that ridicules the views of the moral majority on the right, while giving a magnified voice to the tiny esoteric inner circle of the Marxist minority, on the left.

Our media has always maintained that America's

involvement in Vietnam was wrong and historically irrelevant. After America's withdrawal from Vietnam and president Nixon's resignation, the Communists invaded South Vietnam and started the massacre of millions of people who had been identified, as not being willing to acquiesce in the Marxist ideology of the North. The Left in Hollywood and New York, had been cultivating the notion that only the right-wing has a monopoly on mass-murder, by continually putting all attention on Hitler and the Nazis, while censoring all references to the humanitarian atrocities committed by the Communists. One direct consequence of our left-wing media's campaign to persuade American and other Western countries to ridicule Conservatives and shun the war against the Communists, in Vietnam, was the genocide aftermath, in the Killing Fields in Cambodia.

Spy Game, 2001

When Hollywood makes a movie, it can be about everything under the sun except Communism, so how do you deal with a story, Spy Game (2001), about a CIA agent (Brad Pitt) who gets captured by the Chinese Communists, in China? Simple, you make the whole movie about flashbacks to Vietnam, Beirut and Germany, so you can still have your usual bad guys: Germans, Arabs and last but by no means least, the evil, wicked, mean and nasty C.I.A.; and you don't even need to talk about, the Communist regime in China.

Tony Scott directed and Michael Frost Beckner wrote this white-wash vehicle to illustrate Redford and Pitt's coolness while wearing sunglasses. Old pretty boy

133

Redford is young pretty boy Pitt's controller, who wants to rescue him, before he is executed for espionage by the Chinese Communists. The evil CIA, on the other hand, doesn't want to risk an up-coming trade deal, that the U.S. President is working on, with the Chinese Communist government, so they are looking for excuses to let doll-face Pitt be eaten by the lions, so to speak. So in a film that could justifiably have been made into an expose of Communist humanitarian atrocities, the Beverly Hills left has decided to use it to instead, illustrate the wickedness of the C.I.A., not giving enough support to it's agents.

After all, which is more important; the Communists killing millions of innocent people or the CIA sacrificing a cute pawn, for a political expedient? The flashbacks in the movie are embarrassingly unrealistic, especially the ones in Cold War Germany, which completely neglect to mention the reason for the whole tension, to begin with, the Communist regimes in the Soviet Union and East Germany. These regimes are not even touched-on in this so called "spy thriller". There is absolutely no investment made towards some kind of background story, Redford sends Pitt on a mission to rescue an East German "asset" but, then tells Pitt to drop him, after they are already under way, to the border. This mission is just a side-show for a more important strategic move by Redford, elsewhere in Germany. One shudders to think how people who grew up under Communism, in the former East Germany, who had siblings or loved ones tortured and killed by the Stasi, who are also never mentioned, see this superficial, ideologically twisted bubble-gum piece of film making. What must they think of America? In this film Communism's evils are evaded, unlike films dealing with WWII where the evils of the Nazis are blasted at the audience with both barrels, as in Inglorious Basterds, also starring Brad Pitt.

We swallow this poison because it is jacketed with a nice candy coating. Brutal monsters are played by attractive, witty and humorous avatar-protagonists, such as Ray Liotta, Daniel Day Lewis, Robert DeNiro, Al Pacino, Robert Redford and Paul Newman. The actors, by and large, are not always culpable, in these fraudulent hallucinations; it is the producers and directors, who are responsible and who should be checked. They are talented masters, not only of film making, in general but, also of persuading us to invoke our most primitive instincts, against our own better judgment, to acquiesce in the depravities depicted, as accomplices of intent. We are lured, into the mind of the perpetrator, so as to help cement a bond, which is useful in gaining our loyalty to the poor criminal victim of society, after we leave the cinema. We are supposed to loose respect for our own society, side with the underdog and, above all, vote left-wing!

The Sting, 1973

Wealthy Communists, in the Beverly Hills, who seem to be running things, in Hollywood, tell us, through their celluloid sermons that, it is silly to believe in God but, ask us to accept the notion that there is honor among thieves. In the Sting, East Coast con artists avenge the assassination of a small time black con artist, from the slums of Chicago. The preposterous stupidity of this fairy tale premise is suspended in the film, of course, by Paul Newman's crafty caveat, that "Vengeance is for suckers, kid. I've been

135

grifting for 30 years and I never got any." "Then why are you doing it?" asks Redford. "It seems worthwhile doesn't it?". They aren't con artists, they're grifters. The cynical lie from Hollywood is always, that morality is for losers, while the really smart people, wind up with the cash, in the happy end. They aren't endorsing capitalism, they are trashing ethics and decency, using the audiences own avarice and sense of expediency, as motivation. These ideologues have created a new politically correct establishment, which sanctifies gay marriage, protects the criminal, promotes government encroachment, in our lives and is responsible for the deterioration of traditional values, especially the nuclear family.

The role of aberrant psychology in the "totalitarian code" of political correctness is best summed up by Prof. Heinz Klatt:

"Anyone who becomes politically incorrect by daring to challenge a prohibition of this unwritten code is accused of insensitivity or hate, of being a sexist, racist, a right-winger or even something else. Political correctness shares an intellectual and psychological affinity with totalitarianism. The very term "political correctness" was first used by Vladimir Lenin, the Russian Communist leader, in one of his pre-revolutionary Bolshevik directives. Political correctness is a canon of orthodoxies and prohibitions. It mandates a number of things that we have to accept without question. It is a psychological mixture of the irrational pursuit of certain goals and the process of indoctrination. What is at work is an attempt to purify all of society under the rubric of a secular religion. Society today does not readily allow to be questioned that, all sexual differences (apart from anatomy and physiology) are cultural and undesirable and all cultures are equal and equally meritorious".

136

-Prof. Heinz Klatt is a science professor at the University of Western Ontario who spent two weeks without food, in an East German prison, when he was 10 years old.

Hollywood has been infected, more or less, by influential Marxists, such as Alan J. Pakula, Paddy Chayefsky, Martin Scorsese, John Frankenheimer, Ed Asner, Constantine Costa Gavras, Sidney Lumet and many others, who want to misuse the artists and the medium of film and music, to destroy any faith that remains in our free market economic system, traditional values, religious beliefs, legal system, law enforcement institutions and fundamental ethics and morality, all eggs for the Soviet omelette. These political agitators have been producing an onslaught of propaganda pieces, ostensibly presented as entertainment. They have been obfuscating and trivializing Communist humanitarian atrocities by deliberately distracting our attention from Berlin, China and the Gulag Archipelago. Political documentaries ought to be presented in an objective, un-biased fashion and entertainment movies should not contain covert political indoctrination propaganda. Thankfully the Internet has arrived and honest individuals are no longer dependent for news and information, on the politically charged mass-media or Hollywood. Time Warner and other media dinosaurs are in a panic over the money they are losing, because of pirated music and movies but, there aren't too many tears flowing.

If a movie is described as being political, one is already conditioned to know that this means that it has a left-leaning agenda. Advertisements or reviewers on television don't announce that an up-coming film is left-wing political, they merely say that it is a political movie. Does this mean that there are no right-wing political

137

movies? In the past there have been a few exceptions, far in between such as The Green Berets, The Killing Fields, Red Dawn, Rambo and the very controversial television mini-series Amerika, starring Kris Kristofferson, Sam Neil and Brooke Shields among others, which was available on DVD but, only for a brief window; it is now no longer available. On Amazon.com you can only buy the VHS version but, it costs $400.00, or so because there are only a few used copies left. Why has this film been censored from DVD, if there is clearly such a demand for it?

Silence Of The Lambs, 1991

When two or more souls gather in God's name, miracles can happen. What happens when afflicted minds gather in the name of anxious anticipation? An analogy can be made juxtaposing the movie theater and the church, and contrasting a movie with a mass or sermon. In some cases, enthusiastic disciples are shown how to behave, what to believe and even what to think. Films like "All the President's Men" and "Dirty Harry", are clear political examples of subtle attempts to proselytize a willing congregation of spectators, ostensibly seeking entertainment. Depending on your political orientation, you might feel massaged or offended. But some films transcend the realm of, shall we say, tolerable circumspection.

   In the movie "Silence of the Lambs", the character of Dr. Hannibal Lecter, played by Anthony Hopkins, is put on a pedestal. He is collaterally presented as an artist, a poet and an intellectual genius with canine olfactory faculties, in addition to his more dubious occupation. This has a euphemizing effect, generally, and suggests to nascent

138

predators who may be in the audience, a way of achieving notoriety and perhaps even "greatness".

Considering the fact that a great number of young women and children are in very serious peril every day, and that in all likelihood some will be abducted, raped, tortured and killed, any bane or influence that might, however tenuously, enhance their peril must in all circumstances be checked. Symbols don't automatically manifest themselves with the requisite significance one might ascribe to them, therefore, a director must intentionally compose events that are to be offered up, on the altar of the silver screen. After the young woman in the dark abyss desperately pleads with her captor for her release, in a troubling scene in the film; Hannibal's sadistic protégé in spirit, calmly interrupts his work on a suit made from women's skins to lower a candle fixed to a basket containing food. The poor girl at the bottom of the well is allowed to see the bloodied scratches on the stone wall, evidence of a previous futile struggle. She collapses.

A few weeks after the film had debuted in Toronto, a bulletin was announced on the radio saying that a twelve year old and a fifteen year old boy had raped a *four* year old girl in a changing room at the Cherry Beech swimming pool. One can't help wondering if they had been exalted by "Silence of the Lambs". Had Oliver Stone not been given the opportunity to direct films, perhaps he would have developed into a notorious monster like Hinkley, with violence being the only satisfactory language for his "expression". Peter Sellers was said to transform like a chameleon into his characters, on camera, and off! Strange psycho-metamorphoses on both sides of the lens. Was Jonathan Demme unconsciously fulfilling a desire to punish young women, by having relentlessly lowered Clarice, Jodie Foster's character, into kneeling before Hannibal's abysmal reverie in "Silence of the Lambs"?

Narcissists bathing in their vanity at the Awards deemed this film worthy of Academic citation - there can be little doubt in anyone's mind that "Silence of the Lambs", at least unwittingly, is a sanctification of sadistic brutality. Free speech is one thing, but criminally negligent advertisements for pure cruelty are, quite simply - jet fuel for psychopaths. Familiarity with scenes of cruelty surreptitiously condition us to accept cruelty and the possibly deliberate deterioration of morality in our society. In this instance the prospect of censorship seems compellingly desirable.

Did Oliver Stone's "Natural Born Killers" incite killing sprees? Did the movie "Speed" inspire fire-bombing on the New York subway? It is high time that we listen to specimens like Hinkley; when they confess that they were seduced by films like "Taxi Driver" into acting out dangerous psychotic fantasies. Should no one be held responsible for the contents of these suggestive celluloid sermons? Perhaps Mark Klass is right when he says that America is at war for it's future.

Private companies invest millions of dollars on bite-size commercial productions every year, because they know how effectively torpid viewers can be induced into buying products when they have been suitably motivated. Why should anyone believe that a carefully planned feature length motion picture, would be any less persuasive in triggering eager predators into action?

Some Hollywood celebrity, perhaps it was Barbara

Streisand, coined the expression "fly-over country" to refer to areas of the United States, where the "unimportant nobodies" live. The best way to punish Hollywood for the lies they have been ramming down our throats, for the past five decades or so, is to boycott the movies. Simply stop sending your dollars to these cunning meddlers, who want to destroy our morals and Western civilization. Let's send them a message, from fly-over country, that we are sick and tired of their sanctimonious perjury. Cancel your cable subscriptions and go to local live performances, such as plays and concerts, instead of the movies.

Notes

Chapter 6

Credentials, Regulations And Other Wastes Of Time

The wise will be master of his mind,
the fool it's slave.
Publilius Syrus. 1st c B.C.

143

Regulated To Death

One really good way of slowing down and perhaps even strangling free market enterprise, is to introduce more regulations, in the form of zoning by-laws, building codes, environmental ordinances, safety guidelines, and various price control schemes, (such as Obamacare) all originating in centralized bureaucratic government controlled agencies. Europe is further down this road than we, in North America. In Ontario, Canada, the building code for small buildings, fills a single 4 inch binder. In Germany, the building code fills <u>ten</u> 4 inch binders, three of which are for fire regulations alone. The specifications for building details call for all residences to use a so called "floating slab" construction, made up of no less than 8 layers of materials, two of which are reinforced concrete slabs, in the floor and ceiling sandwich, in order to ensure sound-proofing between floors, and also moisture proofing. In America, we only use this expensive construction, in hospitals and research labs. Therefore the cost of a building in Berlin is four times higher than a building in New York, with equivalent Gross Floor Area. Only the big companies and wealthy people can afford to build, in European countries.

Most of us like there to be rules, which everyone should observe and follow. Since childhood, our experiences playing games have demonstrated to us, the importance of everyone playing fair. Once something is a rule, we therefore defer to it's observance, by default, because of this instinctive assumption, that it is better for the greater good, in the long run. So when we learn of some rule and are informed of the logic behind it, it is sometimes

144

taken by us, to be the gospel truth.

"The rules are: ...there are no rules."

Aristotle Onasis

Engineering, architecture and interior design students learn from early on, that egress doors must always swing out; that is, in the direction of evacuation, in case of fire. This rule seems to be carved in stone. This is true all across North America, and one would expect it, to also be true in Europe, because of the clinching argument of the direction of evacuation. Seems logical. However, the opposite is true in Europe! Why, you might ask?

Germany is the economic power-house of Europe and they have also invented and set most of the standards there, such as the D.I.N. (Deutsche Industrie Normen – German Industrial Standards) known to anyone with a drug prescription from a pharmacist (most drugs come from Germany). During the Second World War Germany was thoroughly bombed and the fire departments in the cities of Hamburg, Berlin, Munich and many others, noticed that many people were trapped and couldn't get out of burning buildings, that had been bombed. They also built their doors swinging out, before the war. Burning buildings begin to fall apart or have chunks, such as pieces of parapet fall down and block the emergency door ways. Had the doors been able to swing in, the people would have been able to climb over the debris and escape. Ergo, all doors must now swing in, in continental Europe.

So you see, that not all rules need to be carved in stone. If such a pervasive assumption as the sacred door swing direction, can be shown to be flawed, then there is a

145

high degree of probability that there are many other rules, which we perhaps don't really need either. How does the saying go? "Rules are meant to be broken". One should be critical of all rules. It could also be argued that since each diametrically opposed swing has a good case backing it up, that therefore, it doesn't really matter, which way the door swings. Most governments are full of agencies with competitive goals, which cancel each other's efforts out, almost surgically. These agencies are a complete and utter waste of tax-payers money. Marxists are keenly aware of this, don't worry.

What a heavy chain around the neck of anyone who wants to build a project. If you want to build anything above grade or below, you will need to get a building permit. This may not be entirely without it's humor value, if you have the stomach and money for it all. There is also a good chance that your project will be in violation of some zoning by-law, in which case you will have to go to a community board hearing, which will cost you a min. of $4,000 in 2015.

Deceptive Credentials

Every rigorous effort is systematically avoided; the disciplines of history, engineering, descriptive geometry, even computer aided drafting, are not taught; all technical skills are especially shunned with ineffable disdain, and any consideration of obeying to objective standards, is demonstratively frowned upon, in Canadian architecture schools. So, one wonders, why the pious concern, that only members of an association with Canadian academic credentials, should be allowed to call themselves "architects". Why should this standard be an exception, when all others are being so proudly ignored? What important benefits do our universities have to offer, to our design students? What are the mechanics behind this serene hypocritical dichotomy? It is as though, the people in charge at the architectural association, want to make sure, that architecture students are, as useless as humanly possible, when they graduate.

The architects of Europe are studied and their work provides a seminal basis for most of the architectural and interior design industry, in North America, even if it is not freely admitted. Sales and marketing are the Molochs of our North American culture, that we must sacrifice all else for. The "business" panacea has pushed the art and craft, out of architecture, in North America. Therefore, the emphasis in design schools has been placed on talk, rather than the intrinsic skills and techniques, of drawing. This has produced generations of design graduates who lack the confidence to design anything from first principles. Most Canadian designers, would go into withdrawal symptoms, if you were to take away, their European magazines and coffee-table books - the primary source, of their "inspiration".

From a business point of view, it is tempting to simply borrow ideas which you know are already good, instead of investing precious time, developing new ones. Pirating ideas out of magazines and pawning them off as one's own is the easy, if fraudulent, way to become financially successful, in the design industry. Most people have no idea how wide-spread and incurable this recidivism has become. Of course, this must be kept secret. For one thing, the pious platitudes about the exclusive qualification associated with academic accreditation, are not served particularly well, by this plagiarism expedient. What do you need an architectural or interior design degree for, if you're just copying out of magazines? And how would renowned clients react, if they were to find out, that the auspicious fees that they have been paying, could easily have been saved by a modest investment, in the purchase of a current European design periodical, since that is where the ideas are ultimately coming from?

Plagiarism neatly falls in line, with "business" expediency. It saves a heck of a lot of time, and you already know the ideas are good; they made it into the magazine, so they must be good! And this has been going on for a long time; when Bruce Goff was fourteen, and started working as a tracer in an architecture office. He remembered that, the partner in charge, secretly eyed a magazine in his desk drawer, before he started to draw anything, on his drafting table. One day, when young Bruce was alone in the office, he snuk a peek in the drawer, and saw that the magazine featured some houses, that Frank Lloyd Wright had designed. When the renowned American architectural firm, Skidmore Owings and Merril started out, in the thirties, they were famous for copying the work of the German architect, Mies van der Rohe. But, since their copies were so lame, Frank Lloyd Wright nicknamed them, "The Three Blind Mies". The schools, the associations and the magazines, were, according to Wright, the three main enemies of architecture, in America.

The work of the American architect, Frank Lloyd Wright, is studied and revered in all architecture schools in Europe. All of the prominent European architects of today, look up to Frank Lloyd Wright as a human treasure worthy of respect and scrutiny. Wright's idea that American architecture magazines are filled with useless mental masturbation, has been accepted and is now held to be true, by most prominent architects in Europe. Although European associations are very doctrinaire, the schools there all teach descriptive geometry, rigorously, as a compulsory subject, for at least four years, and in some design schools, up to five years. Drawing skills are featured, history of art and engineering analysis and design are well covered in deference to "talk". This is especially true on the continent, as opposed to England. In English schools, the issues are discussed at length, before embarking on the design, of a project. Frank Lloyd Wright never studied at an architecture school.

European students are trained to design, conceptually. Although the word is loosely thrown around here, there aren't too many designers, who know what the word "concept" really means. All factors necessary for a design to be successful, must be provided for. If any important factors are neglected, then the organism will not be able to live; the design won't work properly. University Avenue, in Toronto, was intended to be like a Parisian Boulevard. Some of the visual characteristics were provided for, but in zoning the avenue as "prestigious", restaurants, out-door seating and retail functions, which could have helped to animate the venue, were disqualified, in deference to the more auspicious headquarters for insurance companies, banks and hospitals; death was guaranteed. To copy something superficially, without understanding the underlying factors, is to attain only a fragment of the original intent. Intention and purpose are

149

everything, in art and design. Design without purpose, is hollow and unsatisfactory. Plagiarism is also immoral.

Selective Ignorance

World War II celebrations sometimes, seem hagiographic, out of date, and in some cases, somewhat obsessive. A flood of epic movies were made, about the Second World War: The Longest Day, The Great Escape, The Battle of the Bulge, The Battle of Britain, The Bridge on the River Kwai and Where Eagles Dare, to mention just a small fraction. These films were glorifying the actions of American and Allied soldiers, while they demonized the German and Japanese forces. Many documentaries have been made, some more and others less exaggerated, about every conceivable event, in every theater of the war. The dedicated preoccupation with the Holocaust alone, has generated, no less than, two hundred and seventy five feature length films and documentaries. Please forgive if this sounds repetitive but, it is necessary sometimes to emphasize the unjustifiable massive advantage the media gives to the left, and how it distorts our whole perception of the political landscape.

For my generation, the victory of capitalism over communism, and the end of the Cold War, seems equally relevant, more current, and just as worthy of commemoration and documentation. The collapse of the Soviet Union, the evil empire, that was spreading communism, for over seventy years, and murdering tens of millions, if not hundreds of millions, of innocent human beings, in the Gulag Archipelago; seems to be a major

150

historic event, that requires far more attention and scrutiny, than it is now receiving. We grew up through the World War II celebrations of our parents' generation. The fall of the Berlin Wall, is our generation's major historic event, that we have lived through. It seems astonishing, that there is almost no discussion about the Gulag, and the current Chinese Gulag system, that is still executing dissidents. There is also a noticeable absence of concern, for the cathartic events, leading up to the fall of the Berlin Wall.

A wealth of stories about the first cracks, intermediate dislocations, and final crumbling of the façade of Soviet Socialism exists. Events triggered by Stalin's death in 1953, were a first sign, that things were not as stable as they seemed, behind the Iron Curtain. On June 17, in the same year, when the labor production quota was raised in East Germany, the workers in Berlin triggered a widespread uprising, which could only be crushed with the help of Soviet forces. A year after Pierre Trudeau graced the Communist International with his presence, Khrushchev infuriated Mao Tse Tung, by declaring Stalin a mass murderer, at the annual Comintern, in Moscow, which caused the Sino-Soviet split, also in the same year. Mao Tse Tung had been handpicked by Joseph Stalin to take charge, with an iron fist, in China. This Stalinist grounding was a fact lost, on many naïve students in the west, during the sixties. Then came the Hungarian uprising, in 1956, which lasted for quite some time, until it became obvious that, no one was going to help Hungary, and the Soviet tanks were sent in again, to crush the freedom.

There were many other important intervening events, but, in 1979, a Polish Pope was elected at the Vatican. This gave spiritual strength to the Solidarity

151

movement, in Poland, and located as it was, between East Germany and Russia, it also gave East Germans a feeling of hope. Perhaps change would even be possible in East Germany. Eventually, demonstrations sprouted up in Leipzig, Rostock, Dresden and finally, Berlin, until the numbers were too large to ignore. There were many heroes in all these stories, who at the very least, deserve mention. Mikhail Gorbachev was also a hero of this unprecedented epoch. He decided to allow the Berlin Wall to be opened up, to anyone who wanted to leave. Many excellent documentaries have been made about these pivotal events, in France, Germany and Great Britain, but they don't seem to be making it, across the puddle, to our shores. It is almost as though, there is a censorship in effect. We seem to be trapped, in a World War II - time warp!

Some of us have been conditioned, to fall into a contrived obsequious stupor, at the mere mention of Auschwitz; but what percentage of the products, that we buy from Wal-Mart, are produced by doomed dissident inmates, who are being worked to death, in Chinese concentration camps? Where is the outcry from our labor unions, about the jobs that have been wiped out, by the flood of cheap products, which are destroying many manufacturing industries, and exacerbating an already staggering trade deficit? Where is the corresponding enthusiasm and moral concern, about the events surrounding the Cold War? Where are the epic feature length movies, depicting the actions and courage of the new heroes and masses of victims, of this, more recent war? We also have something to celebrate, and be thankful for, in the resilience of our way of life, over the demented, atrocious and bankrupt ideologies of socialism and communism.

Municipal politics is the low-hanging fruit or entry level for people who are interested in politics. Here it is easier to acquire your first experiences as a School Board Trustee, for example before you move up to more influential posts. Some mayors go on to become provincial ministers or Premiere and then perhaps, on to Prime Minister of Canada, if they play their hand well. Normal people, who are not interested in politics because they are pursuing an interesting career or a compatible partner, for example, usually don't even bother to get involved in government. Extremists, on the other hand, who are very motivated by their ideological beliefs, take full advantage of this ladder and so, are disproportionately represented at the local levels of government. But the local level or municipal government is of considerable importance in Canada's most important city, Toronto. After all, roughly half of the Canadian economy breaths in Ontario.

Sometimes, when conditions are favorable for it, an extremist minority, such as the New Democratic Party of Ontario, a communist front party, can actually take over control of Ontario and damage the economy of Canada. This happened back in 1990, when the Liberal base, discouraged by a scandal which had engulfed the incumbent Liberals, decided that instead of voting in the election, they would go off to the cottage. The NDP constituency always shows up in strength, at the voting booth, and they actually won the provincial election. The Conservative constituency was also not highly motivated either, on this particular summer weekend. Because of Bob Ray and his NDP, the whole real estate industry and building industry came to a stand-still. Architecture, interior design and engineering firms had to lay-off

hundreds and then thousands of employees. Many firms
went out of business altogether. Most investors went south,
or over to Eastern Europe, where, ironically, the
Communist regimes had recently fallen (the Berlin Wall
fell on November 9th, 1989) and had given way to freedom
and free market enterprise, once again.

> "We want jobs, not work."
> Banner - Coal miner's union, U.K. - circa 1978

Enter the jovial bobble headed Rob Ford, the popular
conservative Mayor of Toronto. He won a comfortable
victory because he ran on the idea that the government does
not have the right to spend taxpayer's money relentlessly,
with impunity. This appealed to most level headed voters in
the 2010 mayoral election in Toronto, Canada. Rob Ford
had been city councilor since 2000 and found out why the
costs for municipal programs and services were running
sky high, in Toronto. All public servants, staff and workers
belong to the great C.U.P.E. or Canadian Union of Public
Employees, the largest union in Canada representing
around 650,000 workers. CUPE has natural affinities with
all other unions as well, including the CAW - Canadian
Auto Workers, CEP – Communications, Energy and Paper-
workers Union of Canada and is affiliated with the
Canadian Labour Congress, and is it's largest financial
contributor. These unions had been driving up the costs and
threatening to bankrupt the city.

   Few people have the strength to stand up to union
negotiators, who are always chosen for their confrontation-
style aggressiveness. In negotiations with municipal
officials the unions have a good chance of getting what

they want because most officials are nice people who don't like unpleasant confrontations with choleric professional agitators. Besides, it is not the money of the official that is at stake but, rather the taxpayers' of the city. Things get unfair though, when the official negotiating with the union is himself a union sympathizer, such as the previous mayor, David Miller. He simply let them have anything they asked for, or so it seemed during his administration. He raised taxes and held increases of property taxes to 3% per year, while increasing spending by 6% per year. This was too much for most Torontonians. Unions have also sought to increase membership among public service employees for the above mentioned reasons. It is tough negotiating for an increase in wages for private sector employees because the person you are negotiating with will have his profit margin eaten into, by this rise in wages. Public sector negotiators don't have any skin in the game, so to speak because it is the taxpayer's money and not their own. Consequently, the number of bureaucrats has also continually expanded as the years have gone by, further exacerbating an already staggering municipal budget and deficit. This tactic or strategy has been going on, in all cities across North America.

Unions were originally intended to protect workers and employees, especially those doing dangerous jobs, from unfair employers who were taking advantage of their relative hegemony. Why do well salaried government workers, who work indoors, and who also get pensions and cannot get fired, need protection from a union?

Charles Bronson was not a pretty boy actor but, he was as tough as nails and there is not a single second of film where he isn't the quintessential he-man. The French

called him the Magnificent Beast. Rob Ford was also not a
lilly white angel. He was a bit more like a pit-bull with a
football player history and was tough enough to keep things
on an even keel and stand up to these union negotiator
bullies. He wanted to cut spending and shrinking the size of
government is one sure way to achieve this end. He was
like a Canadian version of Scott Walker, governor of the
state of Wisconsin, who also became the main target of the
frenzied media for daring to stand up to the unions, who are
bankrupting the United States of America. Detroit has
already been bankrupted by these unions, pursuing a
similar agenda.

Transit Policy

Subway tunnels are expensive investments however, they
are also powerful catalysts for the economy of a city,
especially when they are planned and installed correctly.
Subways are unencumbered by surface traffic and
precipitation or bad weather and they do not need to follow
the existing street grid. They can and should radiate out
directly to the suburban centers of the city making the ride
for commuters shorter and faster and more convenient.
Subways can therefore be very fast links between the
downtown area and the outer suburbs of a city. This also
has the added benefit of reducing traffic congestion, not
only in the city but also on the highways. Subway stations
are magnets where many people converge in order to use
the system, therefore they are also good places to build
residences and businesses which cater to those residences,
such as restaurants, stores and doctors' and dentists'
practices. Small mini cities have a tendency to grow up

around a subway station, as can be seen around Bloor and Young, St. Clair and Young, Davisville and Young, Eglinton and Young and all the way up the Young line, in Toronto. This can easily be verified, in the view from the C.N. Tower.

Rob Ford was a champion of the subway system rather than supporting the expansion of the tram or streetcar system which only serves to increase traffic congestion, since the street cars must share space with or displace other vehicular traffic. One way to help pay for this subway is to cut spending and decrease the size of government. Taxpayers would rather spend the money on the subway which would make life better for more citizens, than use the money to bloat the already redundantly populated army of bureaucrats who are only working to regulate, coerce and restrict people, who are actually trying to produce wealth and create more jobs.

The Driven Left-Wing Media

The right wing is portrayed or insinuated as having a monopoly on mass murder, by the invocation of Adolph Hitler, when an example needs to be given, of ultimate evil. This benchmark or standard icon of the quintessential pariah, is still invoked routinely by our media, even though it has been demonstrated clearly in "The Black Book of Communism" that Stalin and Mao have had seventeen to twenty times as many inmates murdered, in their death camps, than the six million slaughtered by Hitler in his. Yeltsin opened up the Russian archives to international historians, after the collapse of communism. If there really

157

is a shift towards the right then, this should have been reflected.

Hundreds of feature length movies have been made celebrating the Allied victory in World War II: "The Longest Day", "The Battle of Britain", etc. How many documentaries or movies have been produced by our media about the victory of the free market over communism, or the events that led up to the fall of the Berlin Wall? Where is the corresponding celebration of our victory over the left wing ideology of the former Soviet Union?

Lately our TVs have been telling us that white cops are hunting down young black men and are trying to exterminate them, because we are still suffering from racism, in our society. Rodney King in 1992, Treyvon Martin in 2011? and recently Michael Brown, in 2014. That's 3 blacks in 22 years. Not a very efficient extermination campaign when we compare it to Hitler's 6 million in two years! The carjacking, kidnapping, brutal rape, torture and slayings of Channon Christian 21 and Chris Newsom, 23, on Saturday, January 6, 2007 in Knoxville, Tennessee is a story which was censored from national broadcast by the NBC, ABC, CBS and PBS networks, because the story does not fit in their left-wing narrative of race crimes against blacks. The perpetrators of this horrific crime, were four young black men and one young black woman. Shannon and Chris were kidnapped and brought into a house were they were both gang-raped. Chris was then beaten and forced to walk naked, in the cold night, to the nearby train tracks, where he was shot two times, in the back. They poured gasoline on him and lit him up. Finally, they shot him in the head, to make sure that he was dead. This gang then turned their attention to Shannon, who was being held in the house. They beat her severely, and tortured her for three hours. These perps then poured bleech down her throat, to try to wash away the DNA, which they had left, in her mouth, from multiple oral rapes. Then they poured the rest of the bleech on her wounded body, also in an attempt to clear any traces of DNA evidence. She was then stuffed into 5 garbage bags and tied in a fetal position and dropped into a garbage drum, with the lid closed. There she was left to suffocate in agony, alone in the dark plastic grave, with no way to free herself. As was mentioned above, none of the networks carried this story nationally. None! This heinous incident certainly qualifies as a race crime and as a hate crime, yet the mainstream media decided that it didn't fit in, with their left-wing narrative, of how white cops are exterminating black men. The media is no longer in the business of reporting the facts; they are in the business of spinning the facts and filtering them, to support their ideological superstitions.

Why is it that only right-wing politicians are attacked so ferociously by the mass media? The attacks on Rob Ford aren't the first time the media has behaved, like a drama queen and gone off on a hysterical tantrum throwing episode. Joe McCarthy was a real war hero who fought in World War II as a tail gunner in a Douglas SBD Dauntless dive-bomber, stationed in the Solomon Islands just north-east of Australia. He risked his life fighting against Japanese forces in the Pacific. But when he tried to fight against real clandestine Communism on American soil, he was vilified by the media which distorted and perverted the facts. We now know that Communist agents did infiltrate the government of the United States, during the Second

World War, because America didn't mind sharing information with an ally, in a mutual effort fighting against Imperial Japan and Nazi Germany. Alger Hiss was the highest placed agent for the Soviet Union and was a member of the U. S. delegation at the Yalta Conference, which was essentially a betrayal of the West toward the people of Eastern Europe, who eventually fell under the repression of the Iron Curtain. It was alleged that Hiss was instrumental in giving the Soviets unnecessary concessions which led to this tragic outcome for half the population of Europe. Despite the justification or vindication of McCarthyism, in retrospect – he couldn't prove his allegations and was censured by the United States Senate in the early 50s. To this day, Joe McCarthy is still thought of as a pariah, by many people who let the media do their thinking for them.

In a hauntingly similar attack, to the assault against Rob Ford, the former General Secretary of the United Nations, Kurt Waldheim had to endure an astonishing pre-emptive global firestorm of criticism, throughout the entire Austrian presidential election campaign of 1985, intended to scare Austrians out of voting for him. The pretext for the braying of these New York media donkeys, was his non-existent war crimes, during World War II, in which he served as a 19 year old Sturmabteilung motorcycle courier. Many voters who would normally have voted for the other candidate Kurt Steyrer, switched over to Waldheim, just to spite the media. After he was elected president of Austria, despite all these merciless attacks in the media, his name was cleared by a Jewish historical committee commissioned by the Austrian government, which looked into his case. But this exoneration was only mentioned in the local Viennese news as a small unimportant side story, not worthy of any headlines. This politically motivated media hysteria and obvious character assassination also turned out to be an embarrassing farce.

Governor Scott Walker wanted to eliminate collective bargaining rights for public employees and made $1.5 billion in budget cuts, in the state of Wisconsin, in 2011. This lead to massive protests at the Wisconsin State Capitol, which eventually evolved into a national campaign, organized by the unions, to have him recalled from office through a recall election. Ultimately the voters decided in Scott Walker's favor.

If Justin Trudeau were caught on film snorting cocaine, how would the media react? "What he does in his private life is none of anybody's business." That is how the media reacted to Bill Clinton who made rude advances to any attractive woman in his orbit, even at the office. The media kept repeating that "this doesn't rise to the level of an impeachable offense." And so he was not impeached, even after a string of extra-marital affairs while on the job, under his desk, in the Oval Office, not to mention perjury (lying under oath). Conservatives, on the other hand, are nailed to the cross if they so much as say the wrong thing or twitch in the wrong direction.

The ultimate proof of the left-wing media bias is the remarkable deference paid to the victims of the National Socialists during World War II in the Holocaust mass-murder of six million Jews, beside the noticeable lack of concern for the murder of one hundred million victims of the communists, throughout their reign in the former Soviet Union.

Our media has become an institution which is

161

intertwined with the entire political process and uses it's left-wing bias to try to persuade people, how to vote. It is difficult to imagine our political landscape, without this one-sided psychological programing.

If a movie presents the audience with scenes of people being tortured and portrays the perpetrators in a positive light, then it is safe to say that there is something seriously wrong with the director and producer, of that movie. Whether the torture is being acted out, or the person is genuinely being hurt, as in a snuf film, the intention is the same, to exploit the victim's perceived suffering for the purpose of providing pleasure to the viewer. That anyone could derive pleasure from watching a girl being tortured, is bad enough but, to spend weeks and months investing millions of dollars to refine this kind of monstrosity, can really not have any cheerful outcome.

How many girls were raped, as a direct result of Silence of the Lambs being distributed, world-wide? A girl's body was found near Berlin, Germany, around 1998. She had been skinned. And if you don't think that these movies have that kind of effect, then why do companies pay millions for television commercials? Why have actors been banned from smoking or drinking on T.V. Shows?

Damage Glee (Schadenfreude)
Movie Review - "Election"

In what seems to be a contrived re-writing of a true story, a high school teacher exacts revenge on an attractive young female student, whose affair with another teacher ended precipitously as this other teacher, loses his job over the

162

incident. We of course, are not shown what really happened. One does, however get the distinct feeling that this movie is based on real events because the details are so realistic, like the scene where the protagonist high school teacher, Matthew Broderick is throwing items out of a refrigerator, and is observed by the janitor, from the hallway, just as one of the packages misses the garbage can and splashes onto the newly cleaned floor. Unaware that he was being observed from behind, Broderick continues to throw things out of the fridge, as the janitor quietly moves on, down the hall.

Reese Witherspoon is supposed to be the quintessential perfect girl living in a perfect world, whom we are presumably supposed to despise. The hatred and venom of the entire script and cast are directed precisely on her character, because she is interested in ethics and morality. This, of course, is a no no, in Hollywood. She is beautiful, gets high marks in all of her classes and wishes to run for student council president, because she wants to make sure that things run, down here in her school, as they do upstairs, in Heaven. Broderick's envy is palpable, as he can only watch, from his low-income life-style vantage point (he drives a Ford Fiesta) as Witherspoon enthusiastically begins to organize her campaign.

Now, how can the audience be made to be against this cute little blonde girl, when she is so obviously interested only in doing the right thing? She has to be shown doing something bad, so, in the middle of the film, she tears down her opponents banners, in a school corridor. This is the sole act that can be exploited, by the author, in order to justify the hatred which is thrown at Witherspoon's character. In hindsight, it seems engineered, and not inspired by actual events. Not being able to pin the crime on Witherspoon, Broderick's character throws away some of her supporters' votes and rigs the election, so that Witherspoon loses, although she did get the majority support, which she needed to win. Some of the students, who are involved with the election process and the principal, find out about Broderick's ruse and confront him in the principal's office, where the janitor is also present. Broderick is fired and Witherspoon is made president.

Near the end of the movie Witherspoon is seen meeting with a Republican representative, and getting in to his limousine, ostensibly suggesting that Witherspoon's character is an evil right wing person. This is a major no no in Hollywood; interested in morality, ethics AND a REPUBLICAN!! The Horror.

There are some funny moments in the film, despite it's subversive intentions, as Broderick's character is punished for his infidelities with his friend's wife, when he is stung in the right eye, by a wasp.

Iraq - Unlike Vietnam

There are many differences between Iraq and Vietnam, the only thing they have in common is the fighting. During Vietnam you had a situation where Americans all along thought that, communism was a bad thing and needed to be stopped, although no attacks were committed by any communists on American soil. The prevailing feelings about communism, at this time, were summed up pretty well by the film The Ugly American. However, there were agents in the American Congress and media who had a

164

strong ideological affinity with the left, and so we saw a well-orchestrated media campaign get under way to dissuade Americans that it was a good idea to be involved in Vietnam, and that we should get out.

The very idea of patriotism was trashed by such popular television sitcoms as MASH and All In The Family, where Archie Bunker was made into the laughable archetype for the red-neck anti-communists, that it seemed to become everyone's duty to ridicule. Anyone who had any interest in the military was portrayed as being somehow perverted, almost like a child molester. The prevailing media attitude towards the military was perhaps best captured by the film Doctor Strangelove, in which humor was used to make generals look like warmongering idiots who held us all hostage to their fears and hatred of communism.

In contrast, Iraq almost seems to be the ideological inverse. Americans had been conditioned to acceptance and tolerance of different religions and harbored no animosities against Islam. It was only after a shocking attack on the World Trade Center that the people expected some sort of appropriate military response. The media however had long since been trying to persuade Americans that Islam is somehow misguided, that regime change in the Middle East was desirable and that we should be proud of our military, promoting militarism in movies and television, in such productions as Black Hawk Down, Saving Private Ryan and Pearl Harbor. Patriotism seems to be en-vogue again.

Though the people welcomed an attack on Afghanistan, there was no favorable consensus that the United States should invade Iraq, especially as it seemed to be in total contradiction to what the Europeans were

165

expecting. Most people here in North America have relatives in Europe. We all thought we were supposed to be fighting Al Qaeda, not trying to install democracy in the Middle East and rid the world of Islam! (this arrogance is McCarthyesque!) Today many pundits in the media are trying to persuade Americans that, the right thing to do is stay the course in Iraq and not to leave or "cut and run".

Con Art

You may recall Hans Christian Anderson's fairy tale "The Emperor's New Clothes" about a couple of cunning meddlers who plan to rob a small kingdom of it's riches upon learning of it's inhabitants' legendary gullibility. They invent a magic thread that has the ability of being visible only to those who are fit for their position in society and which requires a supply of jewelry and gold to produce. The king commissions them to weave a wardrobe for him, so that he may know which of his subjects are true. Only one young child is immune to the deception and stupidity which eventually ensue. There couldn't be a more appropriate allegory for the peculiar doings in our trendy art world.

In today's art scene the confidence trick is set up roughly as follows. First an obscure artist's work must be found so that it is inexpensive and therefore easy enough to acquire. It is in the interest of a wealthy tax evader to pay as little as possible and have access to a steady supply of objects on demand. Next, one of his minions puts a piece up for auction at a reputable dealership, such as Sotheby's. He stacks the deck by placing several of his lawyers or other spaniels among the bidding crowd to ensure the price is driven up to the desired level, let's say five million dollars. Our evader cuts a bogus cheque to the seller, in reality his accomplice, for the balance, and a good one for 5% to give to the auctioneer as their transaction fee. The original absurd bagatelle has now been transformed into a five million dollar "Work of Art". The receipt from Sotheby's says so.

Finally, he can make a quarter million dollar cultural donation to the art gallery in his community and deduct three million or so from his income, so that he is in a different tax bracket. He already has the certificate he will need when he files his income tax return. A retinue of professors, appraisers, curators, retainers, and art critic puppets is perpetually preoccupied with the important work of stoking the doublethink nimbus, which has evolved to help maintain and validate this industry of massive fiscal maneuvering, and to shroud the true intentions of these perfidious, though accomplished operators.

Thus, the stage is set for the predicament of the young art student who might feel guilty if he finds himself at a loss to understand the difference between a piece of junk and what passes as "Art" these days in some of the more sophisticated galleries. He might surmise that there is some enigmatic principle behind art that he is perhaps too torpid to fathom, and against the fevered stupor of the art marketing hype, driven by investor imperative, he may, however reluctantly, acquiesce and become a symptomatic fellow traveler. After all, it does feel better to belong rather than go against the majority opinion. Ultimately, he might develop into a champion or even an apostle of this mass psychosis which was, of course, intended to be of avail to the clever tax evasion community.

Anti-reason doesn't need to be justified, it doesn't have to obey to any objectively measurable standard; consequently, fraudulent magnifications of worth, irrespective of intrinsic merit, may be committed with impunity. A kind of arbitrary lawlessness may prevail that allows the deceitful to remain unchallenged and able to change the rules as they go along. If there are no precepts, then none can be invoked in defense of an individual who has no choice but to accept this ineffable subterfuge. Our society is therefore, gradually emptied of meaning and trust.

Chapter 7

Surreptitious Invasion

"Wisdom is expelled, violence rules,
civility is absent, abusive words foment hostility."
Ennius c. 185 B.C.

Potemkin Cities

No one really knows exactly what the population of Red China is because no census has ever been taken, by the government. They don't care. A while back, the Red Chinese government promulgated a policy of one child, to every family, because they were afraid that there were too many people and not enough food to go around. This was around the 1980s or so, perhaps slightly earlier. The best estimate of the population of Red China was calculated by the C.I.A. using satellite photography of the wheat and rice fields, and guessing per-capita food intake. They came up with a figure of between 2 and 3 billion souls. Let us assume conservatively that, the population is 2 billion people. That's almost half the population of the planet!

In your average Communist country, 2 percent of the population were members of the Communist party, and therefore had access to such things as higher education, Western fashion and other luxuries. The vast majority of the population had to live a life of relative squalor, doing mundane, low key jobs and getting slave pay. Promotion was never based on merit, it was only based on ideology or loyalty to the Communist party. Well known examples of this were the leaders of East Germany and Romania, who showered themselves with Western luxuries, in secret 5 star hotels, made by West German and Swiss contractors and suppliers, which could only be used by higher ranking party officials. Erich Honecker, the former leader of East Germany, or General Secretary of the S.E.D. Party (Socialist Unity Party of Germany), as was his official title, drove a West German Daimler-Benz Mercedes stretch limousine, bullet-proof, of course. He went hunting with other Politburo members at one of these exclusive lodges hidden away in a secluded northern forest, inside East Germany. The wives of these tyrants, flew to Paris and Milan, to do their shopping. Everyone was equal but, Party members were more equal.

Getting back to Red China, if we use the 2 percent figure to make an assumption about the population of the party faithful, then we come up with a number of 40 million. That's four times the population of Manhattan, during the day. Another way of looking at it, that is two times the population of the whole of the former East Germany! That's right, the entire population of the most feared Soviet satellite, East Germany, was about 20 million, tops. That is why they have so many nice cities in Red China, boasting luxuries you would expect from a typical Western city. Naive Westerners visit Hangzhou, Shanghai, Shenzhen and (what I defiantly continue to call) Peking and are impressed by the skylines, cars, light shows, Gucci shops, etc., and leap to the conclusion that Red China is perfecting Capitalism, as a kind of hobby, or something like that. There is even a fancy clubhouse in Shenzhen, designed by Richard Meier, one of America's finest architects. Very nice.

Communist countries really have two classes of people: party members and non-party members. One is the upper, ruling class and the other lower class does the unpleasant routine work. You cannot even get into a university, unless your family is clean and your parents are party members. If you ever write or say anything critical of the regime, you can never be a party member. Teachers watch the children carefully, from the earliest age on, for signs of possible dissident parent influence, which puts

171

these candidates on an even more heightened focus for attention. Fear is the tool used to keep everyone under control. If a child blurts something out, that it heard at home then, the teacher sends a report to the political police (in contradistinction to conventional wisdom, they don't have secret police in Communist countries) and the parents will be arrested and interrogated by the political police or state security. If they were party members, their membership will be revoked. In any case they get a criminal record. If their infractions are considered serious enough, they will be sent to a forced labor camp. There is no possibility of appeal, in this type of political system.

One only sees tenement towers sprawled across the landscape in the outskirts of cities like Shenzhen, Peking and Shanghai. The central business district which is conspicuously studded with gleaming office prisms, seems to be daring anyone to challenge their architectural importance. These cities look progressive with their new skylines which boast monumental pieces of architecture like the Central China Television building in Peking, designed by Ole Scheeren in a German branch of the Dutch architectural firm OMA (Office for Metropolitan Architecture founded by Remment Lucas "Rem" Koolhaas professor of architecture at Harvard), which seems to defy gravity, business and common engineering sense. On closer inspection, these super-cities, some of whose populations surpass those of small European countries like Austria and Belgium, seem to have little to no, large green spaces. One imagines life in these mega-cities being similar to an ant's living in an ant colony.

China is a Communist country. 70 percent of all industry is

government run. They have been on a trade-war footing with the world, and are even increasing this pressure, in that they don't allow foreign manufactured products access to their market. To this end they have been aggressively holding down the value of their currency, and out-right barring foreign manufacturers from bringing certain products, into their country. American auto makers have to bring their whole supply chain, over to China, if they want to sell, in China. All manufacturing has to be in China, according to the Communist party.

Large sums of cash that had flown into China, from their trade surplus with America and the West, has been used by China to try to take over American banking power-houses, by buying dividend reserves from such banks as Lehman Brothers, by their four government owned and run state banks. One of these banks, alone had bought $ 270 billion of these "investments", from the now collapsed bank, on Wall Street. So China is a paper tiger that has squandered much of the reserves it had collected, on risky investment decisions.

Before the financial crisis of 2008, the inflation rate, in China was already at 17% and 200 million people were unemployed! If China were to implement a real stimulus package to help their economy, it would only exacerbate this already high inflation and trigger a total depression. China has no interest in helping the world, out of this crisis. The Communists have used slave labor in dissident concentration camps, to win this trade war with us - and have been deliberately holding down the value of their currency, tolerating huge unemployment and inflation rates, stifling their own domestic economy.

The cruel cynicism of their agenda is not so much to

173

further their own economy; it is to destroy the economy of the United States and the West. We have bitten off the cheese bait, enjoying cheap Chinese products, now the guillotine is coming down, on us.

Our naive politicians here in North America think that we can out-smart the Chinese communists. They think that by doing business with the Chinese, ultimately economic forces will be set in motion inside China, which will bring an end to communism by people power. In reality, the Chinese communists are out-witting us – by selling us products and services at dumping prices, they are using our own avarice against us to bring down our capitalist system.

We are committing economic suicide when we selfishly take advantage of their lower prices, by destroying our own manufacturing base and wiping out our small business foundation. What percentage of the products that we buy from Wal-Mart are produced by doomed dissident inmates, who are being worked to death, in Chinese concentration camps? Where is the outcry from our labor unions, about the jobs that have been wiped out, by the flood of cheap products, which are destroying many manufacturing industries, and exacerbating an already staggering trade deficit? Where is the corresponding enthusiasm and moral concern, about the events surrounding the belligerent abuses of human rights in China?

We must boycott Chinese products and services in order to protect our lifestyle and our economic existence. Until there is a level playing field, our politicians should suspend all trade with China. This will give our domestic businesses a fighting chance.

174

Operation Penetration

Only the Czechoslovaks and Hungarians were able, temporarily to buy themselves windows of opening when many people took the opportunity to leave for the West. In Prague, Czechoslovakia, this happened in 1968, from January till August, when the 2000 Soviet tanks rolled in from five Warsaw Pact countries, accompanied by 200,000 troops, to restore communist control.

In Hungary there was an uprising against the communist government, in 1956. It lasted for about one month, during which time hundreds of thousands of Hungarians made the decision to chance a new life in the West. The Soviet Union was reluctant to react too hastily for fear of an American counter reaction, a fear which was to have proven entirely unfounded. Finally the Russian tanks rolled in to crush the freedom.

These were the only incidents where large numbers of non-communist or normal people were able to leave a communist country. It is difficult for Westerners to understand but, in a communist country like Red China, today, not just anyone may leave. Perhaps people from Hong Kong are still allowed to enjoy certain rights and freedoms as a condition of the Hand-over negotiations with the British but, we are seeing many people immigrate to Canada from the mainland with degrees from communist run universities.

You can't even get in to university if there is any question of your loyalty to the communist party, let alone obtain an exit visa to the free West. Only people who have been indoctrinated with an enduring hatred of "Capitalism" since Kindergarten, and who are deemed "clean" members

175

of the party, or are security agents, are ever allowed to leave. We falsely assume that just anybody could leave if they wanted to. People who express an interest in going to America are more likely to wind up in a concentration camp.

What's up with all these Chinese people that one sees everywhere? Back in the seventies, happily, many good Chinese people came to Canada from Hong Kong in order to avoid the Hong Kong hand-over of 1997, when the British were obliged to return ownership of Hong Kong back to China. These people did not want to live under communism. Today, however, we are witnessing a rather large immigration of Chinese nationals into Canada, from communist China, people who are well dressed, polite and avoid all conversations about politics. How could these people get out?

No communist country simply allows people to just leave, if they no longer wish to remain there. North Korea doesn't, Cuba certainly doesn't, and neither did the former east bloc countries of East Germany, Poland, Hungary, Czechoslovakia and Russia. The former head of East Germany's political police, the Stasi, or Staat Sicherheit (State Security) Marcus Wolf said that he had thousands of agents comfortably infiltrated into West Germany, including a hundred or so, in the West German government. He even claimed to have Stasi agents right inside Willi Brandt's office, one of the former SPD chancellors of West Germany. (The chancellor of Germany is the head of state of Germany.)

We know from the Gauck Behoerde or Gauck Authority, commissioned to collect and disseminate all

Stasi files to the victims of their espionage that almost every citizen of East Germany was under surveillance for political behavior. If anyone in your family did or said anything that was deemed to be unacceptable, your chances of getting into university were finished. It would also be impossible to obtain an exit visa for a trip outside the Iron Curtain. Only loyal card carrying members of the communist party, or agents were ever trusted with exit visas to the West.

We also learned from Christopher Andrew's book "The Mitrokhin Archive" that, hundreds of KGB agents had successfully infiltrated large American military contractors such as Boeing, Lockheed and Northrop. They were able to send designs of airplanes and weapons back to the technical division, in the basement of the main KGB building in Moscow. Communist agents working for the KGB were advised to avoid all conversations about politics, especially those that were critical of communism. "Don't think you have to prove you're not a communist by pretending to be anti-communist. This would only draw more attention to you. Just say something like – I'm not interested in politics."

Canada is an open house, with a revolving door, to all the espionage agencies of the world. Canada is conveniently located just beside the United States, enemy number one, for the Chinese communist party. Here agents can practice English, establish themselves in a career which might be a good stepping stone, to a more interesting position with a military contractor or manufacturer of sophisticated industrial equipment or software, in addition to serenely displacing jobs away from Canadians. China has almost destroyed our manufacturing sector, already.

"Many Chinese-Canadian citizens, who immigrated in the 1960s, *entirely agree with you!* They came here, to Canada, and left everything behind, to escape Communism. They love Canada, wouldn't want to be anywhere else, and chose Canada specifically for the values our country represented at the time - values which they strongly feel are now being betrayed. Because they strongly feel that they, are no longer safe in Canada, and wouldn't want me to write anything which could identify them. And that should raise a big red flag to those "tolerant" Canadians who feel we should welcome everyone with open arms and no questions asked - that is, if they are *truly* tolerant people after all.

Some older Chinese-Canadians speak constantly about what they feel is the on-going, and escalating, infiltration into Canada of the Chinese Communist Party. For instance, the Chinese-language news in Canada used to contain well-balanced reporting, with real opposing viewpoints. For some time now they've seen that balanced, Canadian-based Chinese-language reporting has been diminishing, and has now been completely replaced by CCP friendly propaganda. For some time now cards and letters from a relative in China have contained oblique Mao-type quotes, in order to evade ..., well we're not sure what exactly. My in-laws have strongly urged my husband and I to avoid working with Chinese colleagues - especially departments which are overwhelmingly Chinese. And I can tell you for a fact (from personal experience) that, unlike most other races, the stories you've heard about all-Chinese departments in various organizations - particularly financial - are true. I was given a fair degree of latitude because of the ethnicity of my husband. That is until the day they discovered he doesn't speak Chinese, where they then, with open and undisguised disgust, described him as a "banana", yellow on the outside and white on the inside."

So I have to give a great big "THANK YOU!" to everyone at the

Agenda who was involved in the "China on China" program, who had the knowledge, courage, and personal integrity to publicly call one guest on his (suggested but denied) involvement with the Chinese government. I know my in-laws will be forever grateful to you for doing that."

Letter from a friend, who wishes to remain anonymous.

Notes

Chapter 8

Collapse of Communism

"The mills of the gods grind slowly but,
they grind exceedingly fine."
Sextus Empiricus, c. 190 A.D.

181

The Cornerstone of Socialism

Chicanery, coercion and torture, intended to afflict minds with terror, are necessary measures needed to guarantee an effective tool of surveillance and repression, making it possible for a totalitarian regime to stay in power. As long as people are consumed by fear, they will hesitate, even to contemplate resistance. The political police, employing a pervasive network of informants, is the instrument used to commit the crimes against humanity that are needed to maintain a socialist tyranny. This relentless and belligerent intrusion into every aspect of one's personal life is the cornerstone of a closed, forced labor socialism. Incentive is replaced by fear.

Socialism is an attempt to gratify primitive instincts, which have evolved in us over the past four and a half million years. We have lived most of our past as hunter-gatherers, therefore, we are highly optimized as beings who feel good in groups of twenty or so. It would have been necessary for the group, pursuing the common goal of survival, that any useful find should be shared by all, not selfishly hoarded by the discoverer, and that this should be ensured by a strong leader. The feeling of working together toward a mutual good, binds members inside the group. Any outsider would, for the moment, receive the default status of suspect, at the very least. These observations of typical group behavior have been made by anthropologists studying hunter-gatherer tribes in Africa and New Guinea. So, we can identify at least three salient impulsive tendencies of the small group, namely; solidarity, obedience and chauvinism.

First the soviet socialists of Russia, from 1917 on,

182

then, sixteen years later, the national socialists of Germany, from 1933 on, magnified the edicts of the small group and extrapolated them onto a state scale. Although these tribal principles of hunter-gatherer behavior may be good for a group of twenty or so, it doesn't automatically follow that they are still appropriate for a society of millions. In both forms of socialism, workers' solidarity was professed, sharing or altruism imposed, or private property restricted. Rule by command or order replaced the rule of law of the previous political systems, and these new socialisms were severely chauvinistic; people of other ideas or ideologies and races, were treated as hostile, marginalized or even exterminated.

Some journalists in the western media, enchanted by the flower power spirit of the sixties, stubbornly clung to the naive notion that somehow there must be an ideological symmetry of legitimacy between socialism and capitalism. This belief was abetted to a great extent by the spectacle of the diametric face-off between the two "super-powers" on the world stage. But if we take a closer look at these two, obviously different systems, we arrive at the inescapable conclusion that one represents a viable proposal for a decent lifestyle, while the other lead inexorably to a nightmarish existence of slavery in a colossal prison camp; or worse, to mass murder on an industrial scale, around the clock, for seventy two years, in the Gulag Archipelago.

This ostensible symmetry doesn't even hold up if we contrast the secret services of east and west. The Cheka of the Soviet Union, after having gone through numerous euphemistic re-labellings, then finally KGB, the Gestapo of Nazi Germany, and the Stasi of east Germany were primarily intended to enforce political correctness within their respective borders, by targeting and terrorizing their own people, so that they would be paralyzed into reticence by their fear. This directive can not be alleged with respect to the CIA, not informed by mens-rea, an espionage service which collects and analyzes information from all over the world, with the primary intention of detecting potential threats to security from the outside.

Free-market capitalist countries, motivating individuals by incentive, produce resilient economies that are capable of sustaining millions of people at a comparatively high standard of living. Socialist or bureaucratic state-capitalist countries, on the other hand, bring forth government controlled economies with inflation held deliberately high, embezzling people's hard earned savings in connivance; and pursue high taxation policies, driving investors away and extorting their own people. The economic health of a country is indelibly linked to it's position on the ideologically calibrated line between carefully adaptive evolutionary morality in the center, and quick acquiescence to primitive instincts, at the right and left wing extremities.

Despite the fact that the experiment of socialism has been keelhauled by history, there are still cunning meddlers who try to intimidate us with their political correctness. One of the organizers of the uprising, Joachim Gauck, a priest in Rostock, East Germany, said: "We finally decided that it is time to say goodbye, to our fear...then the Berlin Wall fell".

The Berlin Wall

Cold War Germany 1945 - 1989

Fall Of The Berlin Wall

If you are in doubt about what freedom means then, just go to Berlin, the focus of the Cold War, and your confusion will be cleared up. The Berlin Wall was a serpentine ring double-walled structure, completely encircling West Berlin, which itself, was located in the geographical center of East Germany or, as it's communist rulers euphemistically called it: the German Democratic Republic. It's construction, in 1961, ordered by Nikita Khrushchev, was one of two major provocative reactions, precipitated by Kennedy's Bay of Pigs failure, the other one having been the surreptitious deployment of nuclear tipped ballistic missiles to Cuba.

At the end of World War II, in 1945, the Soviet Army quickly advanced into Germany and cruelly lay siege to Berlin and all the lands in the eastern part of Germany, committing a cornucopia of atrocities in the process. Untold hundreds of young women disappeared. The four Allied powers of the United States of America, England, France and Russia together occupied Germany. Berlin was divided into four sectors, one for each Allied army. The Soviet Army occupied the north-eastern sector of the capital, the U.S. Army below, the south-eastern sector, the English the west and the French the north-west. The country was similarly divided into four larger quadrants, and Berlin was entirely located inside the middle of the Russian quadrant of Germany, because the Soviets had been determined to be the first to reach the capital. After much wrangling, the three western allied sectors became known as West Berlin and the relatively large Russian sector, East Berlin.

During the initial organization of the allied

occupation, there was no need for a wall around Berlin because it wouldn't have made much difference where you went within the city, the whole city was isolated deep in the Russian quadrant of Germany, close to the Polish border, anyway. People were preoccupied with clearing away the staggering amount of rubble and debris, and most citizens were skeptical about whether the western powers could even hold on to their little colonial sectors in the heart of East Germany. The first order of business for your woman in the street (men were in short supply), was survival and hoping for news of missing loved ones. The citizens were simply a conquered and hungry people, at the end of a terrifying war, and glad that, at the very least, the bombing had stopped.

As order slowly began to emerge out of the chaos, a conduit road- and railway had been established by the Americans, cutting through the western half of the Russian quadrant, connecting Berlin to West Germany and Tempelhof Airport was back to a routine of sorts. More and more people felt the need to reside in the "Island of West Germany" in the western part of the city. It became increasingly likely that the western powers were here to stay, after all. Many feared the Russian sector, and didn't want to get stuck there should a border become more defined and official. The Russians, disturbed by a tendency for people to migrate to the western sector, put up a wire fence, checkpoints and border guards. By 1946 there was a simple Russian border in place completely enclosing the western sector, and although West Berliners still commuted fairly regularly, they would have to pass through Russian identification checkpoints. A propaganda campaign started to develop between the east and west.

187

On June 23, 1948 Berlin is divided into two different currency zones. Ludwig Erhard's new Deutschmark is an obvious success in West Germany and the western powers felt that it should also be adopted in West Berlin. The capitalist success of this new currency in West Germany, and it's transfer over to West Berlin was too much of a leap for the hopelessly self-styled economy of the east. So, the very next day, the Soviets decided to put a blockade around West Berlin! Unhappily for the West Berliners, the power generating stations were all located in East Germany, and so the electricity to West Berlin was also shut off. This was the beginning of the now famous, Berlin Air Lift campaign. It lasted until September 30, 1949. The German Democratic Republic, in East Germany, was founded shortly afterwards, on October 7, 1949.

From the beginning the communists under Walter Ulbricht denied that there was any communism in East Germany, they named their party the SED, Sozialistische Einheitspartei Deutschlands, or Socialist Unity Party of Germany. Even as early as 1948, while Walter Ulbricht was taking his orders directly from Joseph Stalin himself, the slogan was: "There is no communism in East Germany, we are building a truly socialistic society". We can still hear echoes of this promise coming from Chinese officials and pundits today, in 2015.

By the beginning of the fifties, roughly one thousand people were escaping to West Berlin every year. The government in West Germany passed a law to immediately recognize any East German who makes it to West German soil, especially West Berlin, as a full West German citizen, and they would be issued a passport and be given a thousand Deutschmarks, as starting capital. The communist SED requested that politicians of the western SPD (Social Democratic Party of Germany) or the German equivalent of our Liberal Party here in Canada, do everything they can to disrupt this automatic recognition of escapees, in order to crush peoples hopes in communist East Germany. The SPD acquiesced, being filled with cynical communist friendly idealists, as were many left leaning political parties, elsewhere in the west, such as our own Liberal Party here, under Pierre Elliot Trudeau, the mascot of moral relativism and leftist cynicism.

Joseph Stalin died in 1953 and Nikita Khrushchev became the new General Secretary of the Communist Party of the Soviet Union. This marks a period of relative lightening of spirits, some Gulag gates are opened up and political prisoners released, including Aleksandr Solzhenitsyn. Several years later, Khrushchev himself, would decide that Solzhenitsyn's novel about his own first term in the Gulag system, "One Day In The Life Of Ivan Denisovich" should be published, and Khrushchev would also personally give Solzhenitsyn a literary award, for this book. There was a workers uprising in East Berlin, however, on the 17th of June, 1953, protesting an increase in work quotas, and poor working conditions. The uprising is crushed by Soviet tanks, killing almost a hundred workers and the instigators of the protests are sentenced to death and executed. The world learns that communism will not tolerate strikes, but also that it is not the worker's Utopia that it had claimed to be.

Fidel Castro overthrew the government of Leon Batista in Cuba, in 1959 and installed a communist dictatorship there. In a secret meeting between John F. Kennedy, the CIA and representatives of expatriate Cuban freedom fighters, a raid was planned against Castro's army, to take back Cuba and eliminate the communist regime. Kennedy had promised U.S. air support for the raid, so the 1,500 freedom fighters invaded Cuba, on April 17, 1961. Shortly before the invasion got underway, Kennedy phoned the CIA and told them to cancel the air support. Perhaps Kennedy was affected by the pro-Castro propaganda in the U.S. but, for whatever reason, he reneged on the support. The result was that most freedom fighters were ambushed and slaughtered in the Bay of Pigs in Cuba and some were captured and tortured. Khrushchev interpreted this weakness, as an invitation, to try to install Intercontinental Ballistic Missiles, or ICBMs, on Cuba, the doormat of North America. The continual penetration of East German refugees into the "island" of West Berlin, was also a thorn in Khrushchev's side, which perhaps now, was a good time to redress. Khrushchev ordered Ulbricht to build a hermetic seal around West Berlin on August 13, 1961. Thus the Berlin Wall was erected and border guards were given the order, to shoot to kill, anyone trying to cross over to the West.

By the 1970's, Erich Honecker had replaced Ulbricht as General Secretary and conditions inside East Germany and East Berlin, were abysmal. There was a dissatisfaction with the restrictions on travel, limited rights to free expression, lack of political freedom, the hypocrisy of the media, the shortage of consumer goods in staggering contrast with the West and the deterioration of cities and factories. There was never money available for renovation; all of it was being spent on maintaining the military upkeep of the Iron Curtain, in order to prevent anyone from leaving the Warsaw Pact countries. A member of the Politburo presided over a small empire responsible for all SED media, the Council of Ministers' press office and controlled the news agencies: radio, television, newspapers and all magazines. Every evening this Politburo member would call editors to tell them how the next day's newspapers were to look, how large Erich Honecker's page-one photo had to be and where any unavoidable unpleasant reports should be hidden.

Esoteric think tanks of the Left, in Germany saw the writings of Aleksandr Solzhenitsyn, when his book "The Gulag Archipelago" was first published in 1973, and realized that it would have difficulty recruiting young people, in the future. Intellectuals in Western Europe took great interest in The Gulag Archipelago, and began to shun the ideology behind communism and socialism, in alarming numbers. A new image was needed for their left wing ideology. How could the Communist Manifesto be made more appealing in light of these new revelations about the Gulag system of suppression? Why not simply take every reference to "the working class" and "the worker" in the Communist Manifesto, and replace it with "the environment" and "nature"? Then the color red can be replaced with the color green and instead of calling it the "Worker's Movement", the name should be changed to, the "Green Movement". This new constituency of trees and animals had the added advantage that, they couldn't be interviewed! The bad guys didn't need any replacing, they are still the same capitalist "pigs", corporations and the private sector. And so, the Green Party was born, in Germany in 1975. The environmentalists became the new agitators, for the same old agenda, of giving the government control, over the commanding heights of the economy. The first movie about the Jewish Holocaust, called "The Holocaust", is also released, all over the world, in 1978.

In 1979 the Vatican elected a Polish Pope; Cardinal Karol Wojtyla of Warsaw became Pope John Paul II. This was, in many ways, the beginning of the end of communism, in Europe. East Germany was the Warsaw Pact's most strict and loyal satellite and vital to the Russian economy, so you can imagine the mood inside other less loyal communist satellites such as Hungary or Poland! Poland is located between Russia and Germany, therefore it was a soft buffer that might be exploited by the West, to interrupt the influence of Russia, on East Germany. The Catholic Holy Father's first international visit was, of course, to Warsaw. His parade, on the 2nd of June, through the main street, was to become an event to remember. The whole crowd was possessed of a cathartic anguish, it was difficult to cheer, many were choked up. This produced a surprising quiet in an otherwise impressive number of spectators, on such a large venue. Watching this unbelievable scene from their office windows, one communist official turned to his comrade and said "Today is the day communism died".

Poland became a sign of hope for the people inside East Germany, during the 1980's. News of the Popes miraculous effect and the Solidarity movement, spread through the churches of East Germany, quietly. It was not long before demonstrations started to pop up in Leipzig, Dresden, Berlin and many smaller cities. Things were euphemistically called "the People's this" and "the People's that", such as the Trabant or "planet", a fitting name for the People's car that you could drive around in East Germany but, couldn't really go with, outside the orbit of Soviet influence. So the demonstrators picked a really beautiful slogan for their chant: "Wir sind das Volk" - "We are the people". They repeated this chant loud and clear in every demonstration, it became a stirring and unifying theme. Meanwhile, in Russia, Mikhail Gorbachev was trying out Glasnost and Perestroika, promising more openness and new freedoms.

By the beginning of the 1980s, Ronald Reagan was being accused of being a warmonger because he wanted to start his "Strategic Defense Initiative", a space based defense system intended to intercept ICBMs en route to the North American continent. Anti-war demonstrations sprouted up all over the west, almost always synchronized to take place on the same day. The Union of Concerned Scientists, a group formed in Boston, was skeptical and said in order for a defense against nuclear weapons to be plausible, it had to be 100% effective. None of this deterred Reagan, he knew that even if it was only 60% effective, 60% of the retaliatory fleet could be launched to punish the Soviets for a first strike. It was also clear that due to the layered nature of the flight of an ICBM, that effectiveness was bound to be above 90%.

There are three phases in the flight of an ICBM: the boost phase, the busing phase and finally, the re-entry phase. To save money, the Soviets decided to mount, as many as thirty warheads on a single 240 ton, SS-18 missile. This missile was particularly vulnerable during it's boost phase, due to it's weight and the fact that it was carrying so many warheads! During this phase the missile is accelerating very slowly, making a lot of noise and producing a juicy infra-red light signature. A smart rock is a

10 inch aluminum cylinder, with tail-fins controlled by a cheap microprocessor guidance system. Smart rock swarms, dropped from orbit, could easily home-in on these climbing columns of flammable liquid, rip holes in their delicate skins, causing fuel to leak out and ignite them. Reagan pushed the Soviets into a high tech arms race that, he knew they couldn't win. The Russian economy could barely keep it's factories running, let alone acquiesce in a new array, of technological expenditures.

Hungary was one of the most lenient satellites, of the Soviet Bloc countries. During the 1980s there was more and more dialog, between east and west in general, and Austria and Hungary in particular. On September 10, 1989, the Hungarian government opened it's border, ostensibly to allow people to attend an "East meets West" cultural party, in Austria. Of course, pamphlets had been distributed in East Germany, advertising this "party", well in advance, and more young couples than usual, had decided to vacation in Hungary, that summer. Tens of thousands had reached the West, through the Hungarian border or the West German embassies in Prague, Warsaw and Budapest.

After the fortieth anniversary of the SED regime in East Germany, on Saturday October 7th, 1989, there had been an eruption of protest marches all across East Germany, which had all been put down, violently. Egon Krenz and Guenther Schabowsky, inspired by Gorbachev's Glasnost, and prompted by the people's emotions, decided to stage a quiet coup and remove Erich Honecker from power. Of course, when a new contender for the Secretaryship wanted to eliminate a superior, in the Soviet system, permission had to be given by the Capo di Capi in the Kremlin. Krenz visited Gorbachev, in Moscow, and he got his permission; Honecker was an old Stalinist who couldn't understand Gorbachev's concepts. Honecker was quietly arrested and taken out of his office, but the official version was that Honecker had resigned. The people were not impressed, and mistrusted the new General Secretary, Egon Krenz. This was just more cynical maneuvering, on the part of the SED, because his election was rigged, anyway.

No one took Krenz seriously, so all of his speeches and promises, were simply ignored. Perhaps the spiritually repressed people's indifference, due to a 40 year history of lies, motivated Krenz and Schabovsky to genuinely place faith, in their own new promises, themselves and, make the effort to do something that would convince everyone that, they really meant it this time. During an SED plenary session, Krenz dictated ten points that were to be implemented by the new regime. One of the points on the list, was freedom of emigration. Schabovsky put the list in his blazer pocket. The new regulations were to be announced, on the next day.

The miraculous evening of Thursday, the 9th of November, 1989, started out as a dull SED press conference about the minutiae of today's plenary session, hosted by Guenther Schabovsky. It was a room full of weary journalists, from all over Europe, trying to stay awake through yet another list of SED announcements. Towards the end of the press conference Schabovsky takes the list out of his pocket and begins to read the ten points. Boredom persists. But after he finishes the list, an Italian journalist calmly inquires about the point about freedom of emigration. "When does this new regulation go into effect?" Schabovsky is puzzled, Krenz didn't tell him

195

anything about a schedule, only that he was really serious about it, and that they had to do something drastic, to prove to the people that, they wanted change. So, with a great sense of nervousness, Schabovsky answers: "As far as I know, this is immediate, without delay." The boredom does not subside, to Schabovsky's utter amazement.

This conference had been broadcast live, and what a room full of professional journalists didn't pick up on, the audience at home, certainly did. Some people were in the middle of their diner when Schabovsky uttered those unbelievable words. They dropped their cutlery, piled into their Trabants and drove to the border crossings, by the thousands, to see, if it was true. When they got to the crossings, they saw that the three crossings were closed. The guards at the crossings were surprised and scared at the sight of thousands of people, converging on them, for no apparent reason, at dinner time. When the young guard at the Bornholmer Strasse crossing asked: "what are you all doing here?", the curious crowd reported that Schabovsky's new regulation, had been sent out live on television, that coming and going was, from now on, allowed. The guards were not watching television and, had not been informed of this very recent decision.

The catharsis of emotions is very difficult for Westerners to understand. You have to remember that just trying to leave East Germany was punishable by death. The guards made telephone calls to their superiors at Stasi headquarters, to ask for guidance. Some of the officers, who were on duty at headquarters, knew about Schabovsky's conference, but didn't know what to do about all these people, at the crossings. The acting head of state security, decided to call the Russian Embassy, to get instructions directly from the Soviet authorities, since they were ultimately, in charge of everything, anyway. The Russian ambassador to East Germany, who had also been watching Shabovsky's conference, was equally stupefied and, in turn, decided to call Mikhail Gorbachev, personally, in Moscow, to make sure that he got the correct orders, to pass on to the Guards, at the crossings. The Chinese solution would have been, to bring in the Russian tanks to disperse the crowds and restore order to the situation at these crossings, but Mikhail Gorbachev said to the ambassador that, they should open the gates.

The guards were told that the instructions came directly from Mikhail Gorbachev, so they opened the gates. Suddenly and in unison, the people cheered as they saw the gates being opened and they started to drive and walk through the crossings that, had been menacing them for forty years. Many grown men and women collapsed to their knees when they realized that they had reached the west side, and broke into tears. This was a seismic emotional event in all of Germany, and led to the election of Helmut Kohl's CDU (Cristian Democratic Union, roughly comparable to the Conservatives, in Canada) in the former East Germany, and, of course, in the rest of Germany, as well. Ultimately, communism, in the Soviet Union also collapsed, as a result of the fall of the Berlin Wall. Gorbachev and Krenz had not intended for communism to end, they thought that they could modify it, to make it more humane and fair to the people. Events took on a dynamic of their own, and the people chose total freedom instead. To their credit, Gorbachev and Krenz, could have decided to take another route, and yet, they didn't.

The obvious lesson of the Wall is, of course, it's

197

purpose. If communism was merely a comparable alternative to our capitalist system, then why was the wall needed, at all? The sheer existence of the Wall was proof, that communism was an abysmal system of repression and forced labor. The whole East Bloc was a colossal prison camp, where people had to be incarcerated, in order to coerce them to work, because there was no incentive. If someone still refused to work, or was lacking in enthusiasm, then they ran the risk, of being labeled dissident, and could be sent to the concentration or death camps, where there was no pay, and no protection from harmful chemicals or radioactive materials, such as the Uranium, in the Uranium mines. Dissidents who were sent to mine Uranium, were literally worked to death. Only the healthiest person could hope to last up to 18 months, after entering these mines.

Anti-Fascistisches Schutzwal or Anti-Fascist Protective Wall, was the name given to the Wall by the East German authorities. They told the people that, it was to protect them from the capitalist hordes that, would otherwise invade and destroy their revered socialism. But that didn't explain why people who tried to leave, were shot at, by sharp shooter border guards.

Fortunately, the fall of the Wall transpired relatively peacefully. Unfortunately, the CEO s of the Chinese communist system, saw this collapse, and have been reluctant to soften their hold on the people, in a political sense, fearing a similar unfolding of events.

Chapter 9

The Grand Hoax

"Equality and justice are always sought after by the weak but,
those who hold power, give them no heed."
Aristotle, c. 332 B.C.

Creation and Evolution

The concept of Biblical Creation and the Theory Of Evolution, are mutually exclusive for the imaginatively challenged, only. What atheist scientists deliberately omit, who like to quote Charles Darwin, is that he was a God fearing, eminently pious Christian, who sat on his "The Origin of Species", for five years after he had written it, because he feared that the atheists would misunderstand it, and try to use it, as ammunition against the Church. The Theory of Evolution, first formulated around 1838, was an attempt to understand God's diverse mechanisms of creation.

Just as Thomas Edison could never explain exactly, what electricity really is, and Albert Einstein was also at a loss, to explain precisely what is holding us down, on the surface of our Earth, so too, the Theory Of Evolution, which has quickly become one of the Left's most important sacred cows, cannot explain where anything ultimately comes from. The best we can hope for, is opening the next curtain, in the long chain of discoveries that we think, are unveiling for us, the origin of all things; what Einstein hoped to discover: the Grand Unifying Theory. Many believers in God such as Thomas Aquinas, the Austrian monks who experimented with grafting plants and the French monks who experimented with the domestication of rabbits, had little trouble, reconciling science and the variety of God's universe.

It is bewildering to witness the polarization of "creation theorists" and "evolution theorists" in some southern states, of the United States of America, in recent times. The so called "evolution theorists" are wrong to think that natural selection automatically discounts the existence of a grand Designer. Natural selection could be God's magnificent subroutine, to generate maximum diversity with minimum inventory! Christian theology has always maintained that God gave everyone and all living creatures, a free will, to do what their circumstances and decisions prescribed. Great science doesn't automatically preclude religion. There seems to be a political agenda to push religion, out of education, altogether, and the exponents of this agenda, are trying to use natural selection as a pretext to this end. Religion and science should co-exist in a friendly spirit, and even spring from one another.

The Theory Of Evolution is just a theory but, some scientists believe in it, like the faithful believe in God. Strictly speaking, this goes against the scientific method, which says that evidence must be found, before we jump to conclusions. This theory assumes that life is a coincidence of conditions, energy and chemicals that have been propitiously combined, by pure accident and then evolved, into higher forms, by a process of natural selection. And since the probability of this occurrence is so low, therefore it has taken billions of years to finally, manifest itself. So, if the cosmos can accidentally create nature, given enough time, then surely, an army of determined evo-devo graduates from schools like Harvard, armed with degrees in biology, chemistry or even bio-chemistry, should be able to figure out the formula, in a reasonable amount of time, say fifty years. After all, it only took three years for two guys, James Watson and Francis Crick, to crack the molecule of life, Deoxyribo-Nucleic Acid (D.N.A.) or the Double Helix, in 1953.

The only things that scientists have been able to

create artificially, in the lab, are amino acids. These are fundamental ingredients of proteins, which, in turn are the building blocks of life. In 2004, another ingredient of proteins, peptides have also been created from the 5000 mile/hr impact of a large gas gun. Nobody has succeeded to produce life, in the laboratory, yet. So much for the microcosm.

On the larger scale, left-leaning scientists like Carl Sagan, wanted desperately to find life on other planets, in order to be able to show, once and for all, that life is a relatively simple accident which occurs ubiquitously, throughout the cosmos. Interestingly, no life has been found on any other planet, in our Solar System, yet. Mars has turned out to be a desolate freezing desert of sand and rock, with no oxygen, water or any sign of green or bacteria; and that, is the friendliest place, outside of Earth, so far! The Moon, our nearest alien world, is even less inviting. It is a colossal dead ashtray, with no atmosphere, whatsoever. All astronauts who have walked on it's surface have reported that you are possessed of a profound sense of depression, while there, which cannot be described in words. Every single astronaut who visited the surface of the Moon, had entered into some form of religious faith, when he returned to Earth, in order to help them deal with the intense feeling of hopelessness, which the visit to the Moon had infected them with. Remember that these astronauts were some of the toughest Marine pilots, who were chosen for their ability to master their fear, and remain calm, under pressure.

A living organism must have D.N.A. molecules that are capable of reproduction. A virus is the simplest form of life, which seems to be on the border, as it needs to attach itself to other organisms in order to survive and promulgate. When the double helix reproduces, it splits into two stands and a second new strand is duplicated along each of the previous initial strand halves. How does the D.N.A. molecule know, how to copy these strands? It is as though the little building blocks of the molecule, know how to read and follow blueprints.

Since about 1900, researchers have been endeavoring, in university labs, across the planet, to create the conditions, which might be favorable to the inception, of some kind of simple life form. A good century later, nothing has been able to slither out, of the test tubes, yet. Until it does, the Theory Of Evolution remains, just that, a theory.

If Heisenberg's Particle and Wave Theory of Light can co-exist in physics, despite it's seeming irreconcilability - Einstein refused to accept this dichotomy, but has since been proven wrong - then why can't divine inception co-exist with natural selection and evolution? Carl Jung and C.S. Lewis were both very successful and pre-eminent intellectuals, but they could live with God. Carl Jung kept the door open to the possibility of the existence of God, while C.S. Lewis became our modern world's interpreter of traditional theology, using highly imaginative comparisons and exposing startling hypocrisies. A junior devil being advised by a senior devil, in the thought persuasion, of a believer to become an atheist, was one entertaining anecdote from Lewis' "The Screwtape Letters". He presented our secular world, through the eyes of these clever meddling devils, in a humorous and delightfully witty way. And what of Carl

Sagan's predictions, that there would be life on Venus or Mars? The Bible's account seems more accurate, not only has the Earth turned out to be, the only place we know of, that has any life at all; the abundance, beauty and diversity of life is so overwhelming, on this fragile pale blue dot, that it can bring tears to our eyes.

Where did this idea of evolution come from? Was there an ideological underlay at work here? What previous life experiences did Darwin have, that could have acted as a catalyst for these ideas on the origin of species? As a matter of fact, the book Darwin was reading at bedtime, on the H.M.S. Beagle, during her five year voyage, was "The Wealth of Nations" by Adam Smith, who argued, among other things, that commercial development was a process of "evolution". People selected the political and economic policies, over time, which seemed to bear the most fruit! Far from looking for a way to disprove the existence of God, Darwin was influenced by the common sense of Smith's economic reasoning, in his own ponderings on scientific questions.

In free market economic societies, workers' wages are the highest in the world. That is why many companies are shipping their production over to China, outsourcing jobs. The unions drove the costs of labor up through the roof during the seventies, to the point where only the richest can afford to have their houses renovated, or buy a new car. It is not our economic system which is to blame, but rather our political system, which was more heavily influenced by left-liberal assumptions than conservative values over the last few decades, especially during Pierre Trudeau's despotic reign of socialism disguised as liberalism, in

Canada and the New Deal precipitated by Franklin D. Roosevelt, in the United States.

"To complain that a free economy favors the rich is like complaining that free speech favors the eloquent."
 - Joseph Sobran, Confessions of a Reactionary Utopian

It is only in free market countries, motivated by incentive that, resilient economies are produced that, are capable of sustaining millions of people at a comparatively high standard of living. A casual glance at any socialist country will always show you squalor, poverty, lack of individual freedom and hopelessness.

Incentive vs. Coercion

A free market economy works by leaving people alone, and providing incentives to persuade companies to pursue directions that are considered beneficial. Punishment for waste production is a form of coercion, or using force to compel people into extra work or payment of some fine or taxation. It is the opposite of incentive. This is what forced labor economies such as socialism or communism do, although, in their particular cases (Soviet Union, Warsaw Pact and China), they didn't happen to see any benefit in pursuing a clean environment.

In our open "free speech" society, if one can still call it that, communists don't make honest admissions, they pose as political activists, and try to proselytize as many well intentioned people as they can, using a good cause as a pretext that, has the actual agenda of leading us to a more totalitarian regime. So it is appropriate to single out certain "environmentalists", who don't really care about the environment, just as certain socialists, like Joseph Stalin, didn't really care about the working class. Many true communist ideologues were put on show trials and finally executed by Stalin.

Of course a clean environment is a benefit or value that we should pursue. Just as a fair economy is a value which we must also pursue. How we get there is the question that has produced this chasm between free market and forced labor philosophies. The forced labor direction has killed at least 55 million inmates in the Gulag Archipelago, under Stalin, during peace time (Methvin, National Review, Sept. 1989, pg. 52). Where is the concern about these and other communist crimes?

Look behind the facade, and be more discriminatory, before you fall for someone, hook, line and sinker. There is such a thing as deception.

The Unholy Trinity

Karl Marx, Sigmund Freud and Albert Einstein, all from the German speaking countries of Prussia, Austria and Switzerland respectively, ushered socialism/communism, atheism and relativity/relativism, into the twentieth century. This lead to two world wars and the biggest slaughter of human life in history, the victims numbering in the hundreds of millions. No one knows, even unto this day, how many millions were worked to death, in the soviet Gulag of Stalin or the concentration camps of Mao Tse

Tung, Joseph Stalin's hand-picked protégé – not to mention the mass murders in Cambodia, Laos, Korea and Vietnam, and most of the countries of Africa, all in the name of socialism or Marxism.

Also remember that Albert Einstein wrote a letter to President Truman, pleading with him to start the development of the Atom Bomb. This ultimately led to the incineration of a quarter of a million, or more Japanese civilians, in the non-military or "soft" targets of the cities of Nagasaki and Hiroshima, in 1945.

Socialism has been tried in a hundred and fifty countries during the twentieth century; and it has failed everywhere. So you're Chomskyesque rebuttal is: "That wasn't the *real* socialism."

Well, if those were the runners up, I don't want to see what the *real* socialism will bring.

Voter Apathy

Of course low voter turn-out is a bad thing but, why blame the electorate? It should be seen for what it is – a clear statement about the state of our political affairs. The vast majority of political decisions are made behind closed doors, by a very tiny minority of people called parliamentarians or representatives. And their decisions are then processed and pasteurized by an army of a bureaucracy called government, who are really catering to lobbyists and special interest groups. These bureaucrats and lobbyists don't get voted into power by we the people.

Special interest groups have a disproportionately high influence on our political policies, while the electorate senses that we have a disproportionately low influence on the decisions that are made. Every once in a while, we get to choose which light bulb is screwed onto the tip of the Christmas tree.

The reality is that we are being treated like kindergarten children by a political elite who thinks it knows better. A majority of citizens would probably prefer the death sentence for predators who torture and kill women and children or, that we should not send troops to Afghanistan, for example. Our governments, on the other hand, have made up their minds on these issues, long ago, and that's that.

We fought for a century about whether the government should control the economy, as in Nazi Germany and Soviet Russia, or whether free people should control their own lives. The planners professed altruism for the working class then, and as we learned from the Gulag Archipelago, this concern was a lie. Now, the planners are re-emerging as "environmentalists" who profess concern for the ecology of our planet.

The Grand Hoax

One of the great fallacies of our times was, and for the uninformed, still is, the existence of "socialism". There is no such thing. Socialism is only a delusive but seductive Marxian catchword, a euphemism for the bitter reality of the over-bureaucratized, monopolistic and oppressive communism or state-capitalism. The attractive word "socialism" seems to imply special regard for one's socii (plural of the Latin word socius, eg. Associate), for one's fellow human beings. It implies, one would believe, respect for human values, human achievements, for common decency, for human integrity, and particularly for human life. How well the "socii" did really fare under socialism, is illustrated by the record of the human rights violations, to use a mild expression, of the socialist fatherland; Moscow sources put the total number of victims, deaths that is, "liquidated" to use the Soviet term, since 1917, under Lenin's and Stalin's "peace" conditions (excluding the WWII casualties), to over 50 million men, women and children. The "respect" for human life was recently demonstrated in Red China: the June 3-4, 1989 massacre of unarmed male and female students in Tiananmen Square and, in front of running TV cameras. Ironically, the Berlin Wall collapsed 5 months later.

But let us concentrate on the economic aspects of socialism. It is obvious to any person with a bit of common sense, that in the highly complex industrialized world of the 21st century, no other economy can be viable, but a capitalist economy. Capital correctly referring to the accumulated resources (saved best, and not borrowed) needed and available, for economic, social and cultural development. Without capital, development is impossible. The crucial question is, who owns or directs or decides on the deployment, of the capital goods, tools and investments? Are the significant decisions distributed among a number of competing, therefore efficiency conscious groups, "firms" in a pluralistic manner of a free market society, in a tolerant democracy or, are all capital goods and tools concentrated (all the various media of communications and the police forces, so called "security" forces included) monopolized in the hands of only <u>one</u> group or "party"? As we know, this monopole-party is claiming all the know-how and expertise (without base and wrongfully, of course), claiming also the monopoly of virtue – in the name of "liberty" (whatever they mean by that), "equality" (except, keeping all the privileges and wealth for themselves, for the "deserving" nomenclatura) and "fraternity" (of the unionized comrades only, of course), creating an over-bureaucratized, over-centralized, featherbedding, corrupt (and inherently so), and therefore inefficient economic system. This economic system is complemented by a one party dominated totalitarian political system, to keep this economic anomaly going. In other words, we are contrasting between either a free-market "capitalist" pluralistic economic order or, a regimented, bureaucracy directed state-capitalism of socialists. But both systems are "capitalist" systems by necessity. However, the pluralist social order still accords choice, or at least some leeway for the individual. In comparison, the monolithic totalitarian, allegedly non-discriminating, but pigeonholing system of "planned" socialism is taking away the choice from the individual, where everything is being prescribed, regulated, regimented, controlled and legislated for the "common good". Who defines and decides what this common good is? The party decides, of course. The monopolistic central party defines the common good. There remains little choice, from the cradle to the grave, for the individual in socialism, but to obey, to follow obsequiously, the "advice" of the party.

As to the question, which system is viable, there is no further argument needed: millions have voted with their feet. The flow of refugees is, and has always been, underlined!unidirectional! The economic aid was needed, after 70 years of "glorious socialism" in the Soviet Union, the fatherland of communism, not for the West, which had to send that aid to Russia, despite the prediction of Karl Marx that the capitalist West was doomed to collapse. Sapienti sat.

Some Rhodes scholars still don't grasp it.

"The goal of Socialism is Communism."

- Vladimir Lenin, founder of the Soviet Union

"America is like a healthy body and it's resistance is threefold: it's patriotism, it's morality and it's spiritual life. If we can undermine these three areas, America will collapse from within."

- Joseph Stalin, biggest murderer in human history

Notes

Bibliography

ETHOS – Motivation (in chronological order)

MISES, Ludwig von   HUMAN ACTION
1949, Yale University Press, Henry Regnery Company,
Free Market Enterprise incentives, deterrents and re
wards. An Austrian School of Economics classic.

CHAMBERS, Whittaker   WITNESS
1952, Washington D.C., Regnery Gateway, Eye-wit-
ness account of Soviet infiltration in U.S. government.

SKOUSEN, Dr. W. Cleon   THE NAKED COMMUNIST
1958, Izzard Ink Publishing, The agenda of the
Communist Party of the United States of America.

SOLZHENITSYN, Aleksandr   THE GULAG ARCHIPELAGO
1973, Harper & Row Publishers Inc. Account of the
industrial scale mass-murder, in the Soviet Union.

HAYEK, Friedrich von   THE FATAL CONCEIT
1988, University of Chicago, Routledge, London, A
thesis on the assumptions and errors of Socialism.

GAIRDNER, William D. THE WAR AGAINST THE FAMILY
1992, Toronto, Stoddart publishing Co. Limited,
Deliberate government erosion of the traditional family.

ANDREW, Christopher   THE MITROKHIN ARCHIVE
1999, London, Penguin Books, K.G.B. psychological
warfare & espionage against the West.

FINKELSTEIN, Norman   THE HOLOCAUST INDUSTRY
2000, London, Verso, Reflections on the exploitation of
Jewish suffering.

LOUDON, Trevor   BARACK OBAMA AND THE
ENEMIES WITHIN
2011, Pacific Freedom Foundation, Las Vegas,
Encyclopedia of the Marxist networks in the U.S.A.

LOGOS – Learning (in chronological order)

WATSON, James D.   THE DOUBLE HELIX
1968, A Mentor Book, A personal account of the
discovery of the structure of D.N.A.

DARWIN, Charles   THE ILLUSTRATED ORIGIN
OF SPECIES
1979, New York, Hill and Wang (Farrar, Straus and
Giroux) The Theory of Evolution with illustrations.

TELLER, Edward   ENERGY
1979, San Francisco, W. H. Freeman and Company,
The superstitions of the Environmental movement.

SAGAN, Carl   COSMOS
1980, New York, Random House, An illustrated thesis
outlining human knowledge, up to 1978.

JASTROW, Robert   HOW TO MAKE NUCLEAR
WEAPONS OBSLETE
1983, Little, Brown & Company, Boston, Strategic De-
fence Initiative succinctly explained.

GILDER, George   THE SPIRIT OF ENTERPRISE
1984, Institute for Contemporary Studies Press,
Why government interferes with prosperity.

UNDERWOOD, Chuck   THE GENERATIONAL
IMPERATIVE
2007, Charleston, BookSurge, An insightful comparison of values of Silent through Millennial generations.

EROS – Perception (in chronological order)

DILLE, John   BAY OF PIGS
1963, magazine article, LIFE Magazine, The reason for
the Cuban Missile Crisis and the Berlin Wall, in 1961.

STEVENS, Geoffrey   TRUDEAU ONCE ON BLACKLIST
1968, newspaper article, Ottawa, Globe and Mail,
Pierre Elliott Trudeau's complacent involvement with
the Comintern.

SCANLON & GROSS   THE BOOK OF ALIEN
1979, Heavy Metal Communications Inc. The making
of the Ridley Scott film: Alien.

SMITH, Thomas G.   INDUSTRIAL LIGHT AND MAGIC
1986, Del Rey (Ballantine Books), The art of special
effects, behind the scenes.

GRENIER, Richard   CAPTURING THE CULTURE
1990, Lanham, MD, Ethics and Public Policy Center,
Political propaganda hidden in cinema, during the 1980s.

SHAPIRO, Ben   PRIMETIME PROPAGANDA
2011, Broadside Books,   Overdue exposé of Marxist
proselytization in Hollywood produced T.V. shows.

Notes